EYEWITNESS GUIDES

AMPHIBIAN

Underside of
neotenous alpine newt

Tiger salamander

European common frog
preparing for take-off

EYEWITNESS GUIDES
AMPHIBIAN

Mantellas showing colour variations

Mantellas

Written by
DR. BARRY CLARKE

Photographed by
GEOFF BRIGHTLING and
FRANK GREENAWAY

Great crested newt tadpole

African bullfrog

DORLING KINDERSLEY
London • New York • Stuttgart

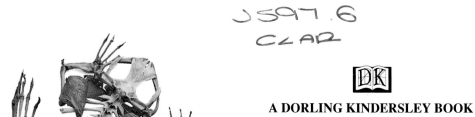

DK

A DORLING KINDERSLEY BOOK

Project editor Marion Dent
Art editor Jill Plank
Managing editor Helen Parker
Managing art editor Julia Harris
Production Louise Barratt
Picture research Clive Webster
Extra photography Mike Linley

This Eyewitness ® Guide has been conceived by
Dorling Kindersley Limited
and Editions Gallimard

First published in Great Britain in 1993 by
Dorling Kindersley Limited,
9 Henrietta Street, London WC2E 8PS

A CIP catalogue record for this book is
available from the British Library

ISBN 0 7513 6004 X

Colour reproduction by Colourscan, Singapore
Printed in Singapore by Toppan

Skeleton of
Surinam
toad

Poison-dart frog

Cane toad

Red-eyed
treefrog
on leaf

Jeremy Fisher from
Beatrix Potter's
(1866–1943) *The
Tale of Mr.
Jeremy Fisher*

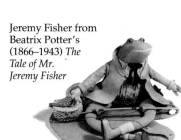

Walking
sequence of a
tiger salamander

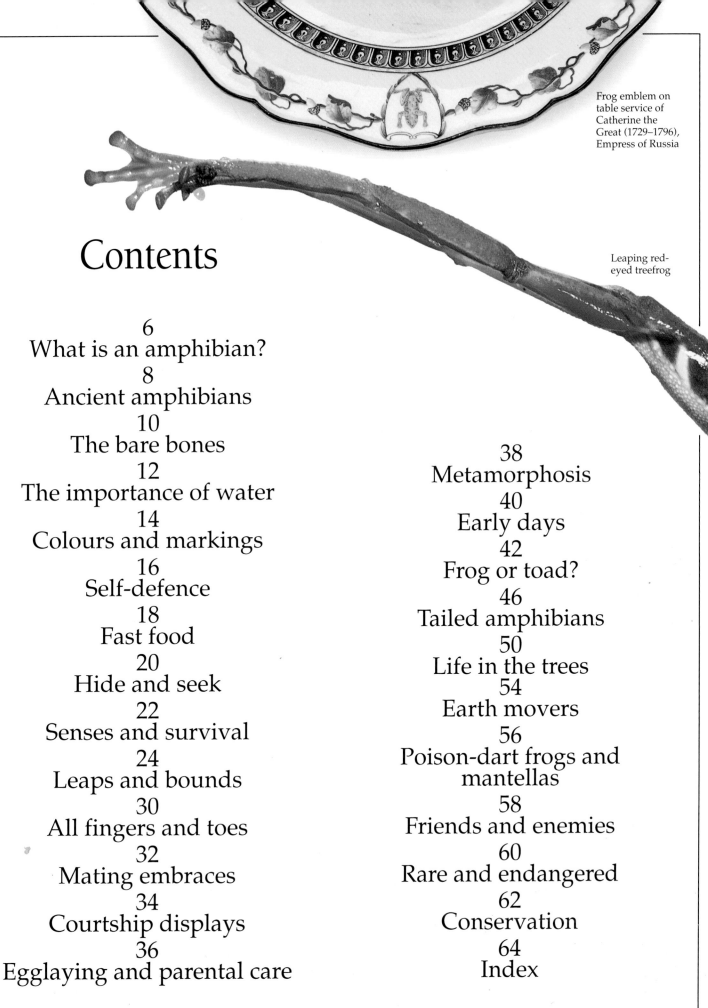

Frog emblem on table service of Catherine the Great (1729–1796), Empress of Russia

Leaping red-eyed treefrog

Contents

What is an amphibian?

LIVING AMPHIBIANS are divided into three groups – frogs and toads, newts, salamanders, and sirens, and the little-known, worm-like caecilians. Amphibians are vertebrates (animals that have a backbone) like fish, reptiles, birds, and mammals. They are cold-blooded, which means that their body temperature varies with their surroundings. Unlike warm-blooded animals (mammals and birds) amphibians do not need to eat frequently to maintain their body temperature, so their food intake increases or decreases with their temperature and activity level. Amphibians have a naked skin (lacking hair, feathers, or surface scales), and can breathe through their skin as well as, or instead of, their lungs.

IN AND OUT OF WATER
This amphibious car can be driven on land or in water. The words "amphibious" and "amphibian" come from the Greek *amphi* and *bios* meaning "double life", that is, they can live or function on land and in water. Most amphibians pass from a free-living, aquatic (in water), larval stage into a terrestrial (land-based) adult.

Skin of square-marked toad (above)

Skin of tree-frog (right)

ONLY SKIN DEEP
An amphibian's skin is very special. Like all amphibians, frogs and toads use it to breathe, lose or take up water, produce colour patterns and markings for defence (pp. 20–21), and to attract a mate (pp. 32–33). They also secrete mucus from their skin to keep it moist and prevent damage to the skin's outer layer.

A European common frog lives in woodlands close to water and ranges in length from 6–10 cm (2.5–4 in)

FROG-SHAPED
Frogs and toads (pp. 42–45) have a distinctive body shape – a large head with a wide mouth, prominent eyes, a rather fat body, no tail, back legs longer than the front ones, and an "extra" (third) heel section to the leg above the long foot. They probably evolved these features to chase, jump after, or lunge at their diet of insects on the move (pp. 18–19).

Smooth, slimy skin of frog is typical

Fire salamander's markings display polymorphism

What is not an amphibian?

This tegu lizard from the tropical parts of South America looks similar to a salamander, such as the fire salamander (below), and some snakes, particularly the little worm snakes, look like caecilians, but lizards and snakes are reptiles, not amphibians. Reptiles can easily be told apart from amphibians by their dry, scaly skin. Earthworms and caecilians certainly look very similar, but many a biologist has been startled to see the worm they had picked up, open its mouth to show an impressive set of curved, sharp, little teeth! Also, some tadpoles look like small fish, but the lack of scales and body fins shows that they are quite different.

Tegu lizard – not an amphibian

Skin of great crested newt

Skin of mandarin salamander

THE ROUGH AND THE SMOOTH
Typically, newts have smooth, slimy skin while salamanders have dry, warty skin, but this is no more true than the same difference in frogs and toads. There are always exceptions, as with the fire salamander (bottom), which feels smooth and damp.

Typical dry, scaly skin of reptile

ODD AMPHIBIAN
The body rings on a caecilian make it look like a worm, but the shark-like head and needle-sharp teeth show it is no worm! Some species have tiny, fish-like scales within the rings. About 170 species are found in tropical parts of the world.

European fire salamander lives in forests, but near water, and ranges in length from 15–32 cm (6–13 in)

Fire salamander's smooth, damp skin is typical of many amphibians

ANCESTRAL SHAPE
Newts and salamanders (pp. 46–49) are more like the early ancestral amphibians than either the more distinctive frogs and toads, or the caecilians – the overall body shape has remained basically the same (pp. 8–9). The head is narrow with smaller eyes and a smaller mouth than in frogs and toads; the body is longer and more lizard-shaped; and there is always a well-developed tail. The legs are similar in size and length, so they walk slowly to moderately fast, and catch slow-moving insects and earthworms for their food (pp. 18–19).

Ancient amphibians

THE FIRST AMPHIBIANS appeared some 360 million years ago during the Devonian period. They evolved from fishes with fleshy, lobed fins that looked like legs, and, like *Ichthyostega*, had fish-like features. Like their ancestors, they may have been attracted onto land by a good supply of food and relatively few enemies (pp. 58–59) to prey on them. While their ancestors had lungs for breathing air and began using their lobed fins for moving around on land, the early amphibians developed efficient walking limbs. The Great Age of amphibians was from the Devonian to the Permian periods, when they were more varied in size and shape than they are today. *Diplocaulus*, for example, was quite small, while *Eryops* grew to 2 m (6.5 ft) or more. Most amphibians had become extinct by the Triassic period, leaving only a few – such as *Triadobatrachus* and *Rana pueyoi* – to evolve into modern amphibians (pp. 42–49).

TOAD IN THE HOLE
This toad is not a fossil – it is mummified. When it was tiny, the toad entered this hollow stone (found in England in the 1890s) via a small hole at one end, but eventually it died from a lack of food, water, and air.

Artist's reconstruction of *Triadobatrachus*

Short hind leg

One-half of *Triadobatrachus* fossil

FISHY FINS
These are reconstructions of *Ichthyostega*, an early amphibian from the Devonian period in Greenland. It had some fish-like features, such as a tail fin and small scales, in its distinctly amphibian body, but had fewer skull bones and legs suitable for walking.

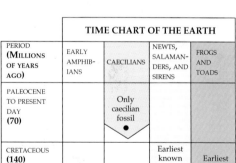
Skeleton of *Ichthyostega*

Reconstruction of *Ichthyostega*

TIME CHART OF THE EARTH				
PERIOD (MILLIONS OF YEARS AGO)	EARLY AMPHIBIANS	CAECILIANS	NEWTS, SALAMANDERS, AND SIRENS	FROGS AND TOADS
PALEOCENE TO PRESENT DAY (70)		Only caecilian fossil ●		
CRETACEOUS (140)			Earliest known salamander	Earliest known frog
JURASSIC (190)			◇ ●	●
TRIASSIC (225)				●
PERMIAN (270)	*Eryops* ●			*Triadobatrachus*
CARBONIFEROUS (350)	*Ichthyostega*			
DEVONIAN (400)	◇◇			

Duration of each period not to scale

Sharp teeth of a meat eater

Skeleton of *Eryops*

AMPHIBIAN CROCODILE
This skeleton is of *Eryops*, a crocodile-like amphibian which lived in swamps in Texas in the southern USA during the Permian period. These terrestrial creatures used their strong limbs to move around on land.

Wide, flat
skull, like
modern
frogs

Short
tail

ANCIENT FROG
This 20-million-year-old fossil frog, *Discoglossus*, is from
the Miocene period and was found in Germany. It is
structurally similar to its close relative from the late
Jurassic period, *Eodiscoglossus*, which was found in
Spain. The modern living species of *Discoglossus*
show that they have remained almost unchanged
over the last 150 million years.

Outline
of skeleton

SLIM EVIDENCE
This fossil sandwich
(above and left) is the
only known specimen
of *Triadobatrachus*,
which was found in
France, dating from
the Triassic period
about 210 million
years ago. It has a
wide, flat, frog-like
skull, but contains
more vertebrae than
modern frogs do, and
also has a bony tail
and short, hind legs.

MORE MODERN FROG
Well-preserved fossil frog skeletons, like *Rana pueyoi*
from the Miocene of Spain, are very like the modern
European frogs which belong to the same genus, *Rana*
(pp. 42–43). Fossil frogs like this help experts to date
when modern frog groups first appeared. They also
show how little some groups have changed in the last
25 million years since the early Miocene period.

Fleshy,
long
hind leg

Body shape
of fossil
salamander
like that of
modern
hellbender

RELATIVE FROM ABROAD
This fossil salamander, whose Latin name is
Cryptobranchus scheuchzeri, was found in Switzer-
land and is about eight million years old. It is a
close relative of the hellbender, *Cryptobranchus
alleganiensis*, the only living member now found
in the southeastern USA. Fossils like this provide evidence that some amphibians, like these
hellbenders (pp. 48–49), once had a much wider
distribution and that land masses that are now
separate were once joined. Unfortunately, the
fossil record is poor and their origins and
relationship remain a mystery.

Short, stout
leg supporting
heavy body

ARROW-HEADED AMPHIBIAN
This odd-looking amphibian is
Diplocaulus (60 cm, 24 in long), a
member of an extinct group which
lived in Permian ponds in Texas, USA.

The bare bones

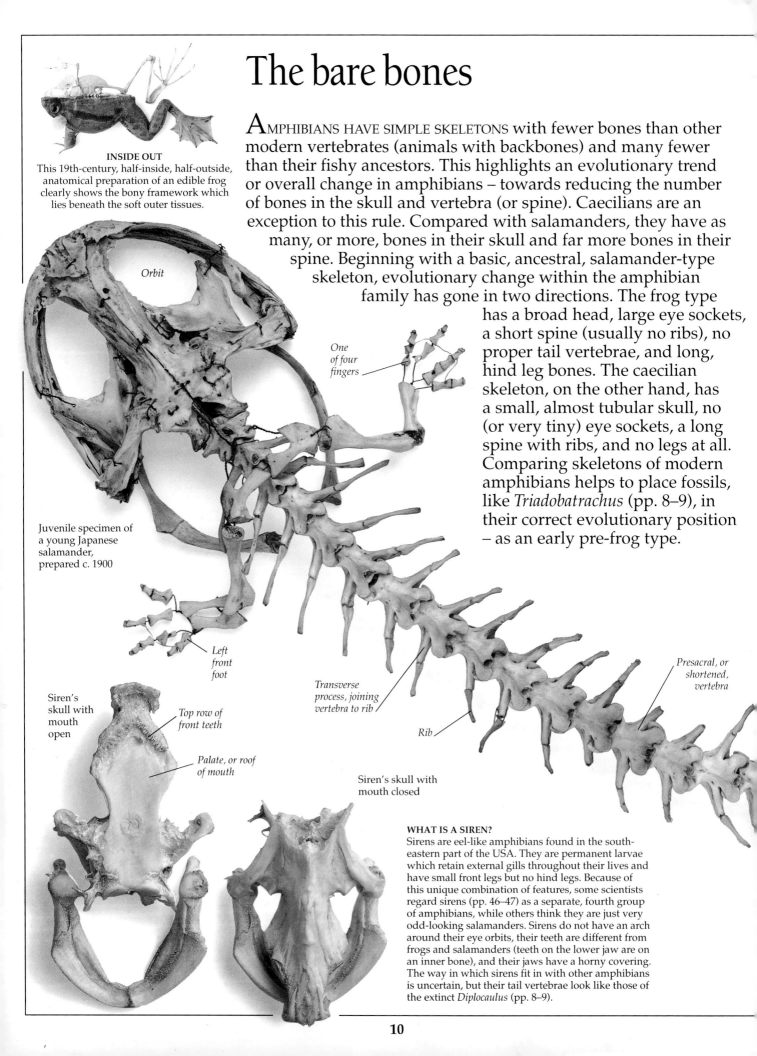

INSIDE OUT
This 19th-century, half-inside, half-outside, anatomical preparation of an edible frog clearly shows the bony framework which lies beneath the soft outer tissues.

AMPHIBIANS HAVE SIMPLE SKELETONS with fewer bones than other modern vertebrates (animals with backbones) and many fewer than their fishy ancestors. This highlights an evolutionary trend or overall change in amphibians – towards reducing the number of bones in the skull and vertebra (or spine). Caecilians are an exception to this rule. Compared with salamanders, they have as many, or more, bones in their skull and far more bones in their spine. Beginning with a basic, ancestral, salamander-type skeleton, evolutionary change within the amphibian family has gone in two directions. The frog type has a broad head, large eye sockets, a short spine (usually no ribs), no proper tail vertebrae, and long, hind leg bones. The caecilian skeleton, on the other hand, has a small, almost tubular skull, no (or very tiny) eye sockets, a long spine with ribs, and no legs at all. Comparing skeletons of modern amphibians helps to place fossils, like *Triadobatrachus* (pp. 8–9), in their correct evolutionary position – as an early pre-frog type.

Orbit

One of four fingers

Juvenile specimen of a young Japanese salamander, prepared c. 1900

Left front foot

Transverse process, joining vertebra to rib

Rib

Presacral, or shortened, vertebra

Siren's skull with mouth open

Top row of front teeth

Palate, or roof of mouth

Siren's skull with mouth closed

WHAT IS A SIREN?
Sirens are eel-like amphibians found in the south-eastern part of the USA. They are permanent larvae which retain external gills throughout their lives and have small front legs but no hind legs. Because of this unique combination of features, some scientists regard sirens (pp. 46–47) as a separate, fourth group of amphibians, while others think they are just very odd-looking salamanders. Sirens do not have an arch around their eye orbits, their teeth are different from frogs and salamanders (teeth on the lower jaw are on an inner bone), and their jaws have a horny covering. The way in which sirens fit in with other amphibians is uncertain, but their tail vertebrae look like those of the extinct *Diplocaulus* (pp. 8–9).

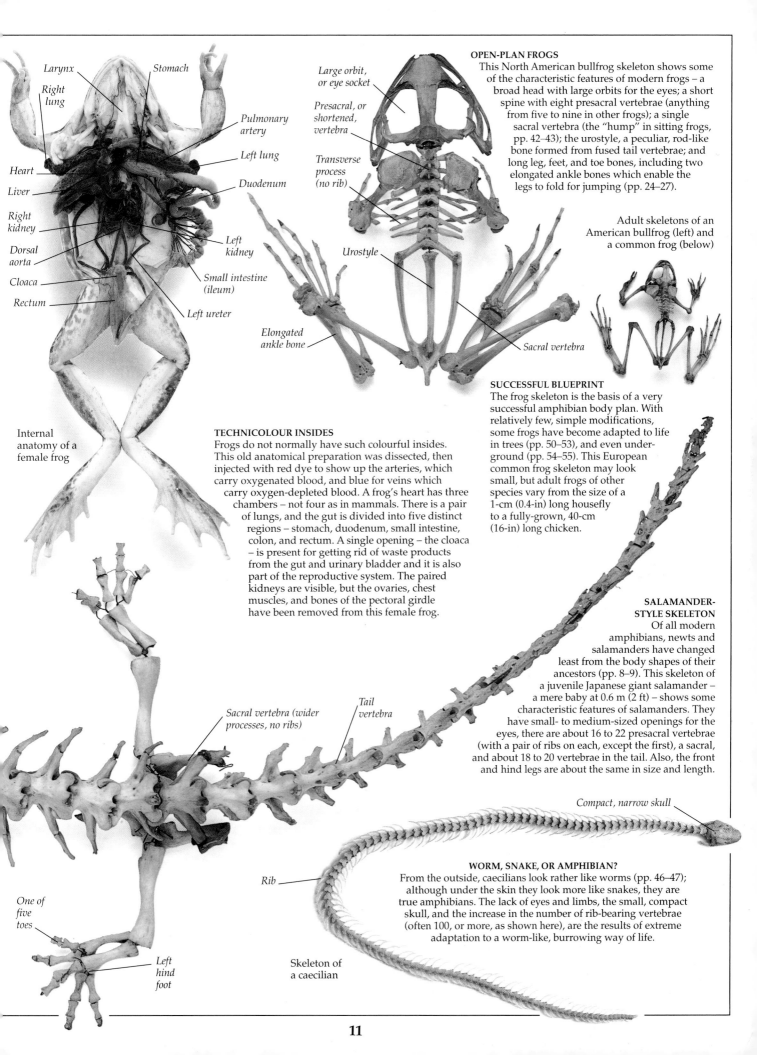

Larynx

Stomach

Right lung

Pulmonary artery

Left lung

Heart

Duodenum

Liver

Right kidney

Left kidney

Dorsal aorta

Small intestine (ileum)

Cloaca

Rectum

Left ureter

Internal anatomy of a female frog

OPEN-PLAN FROGS
This North American bullfrog skeleton shows some of the characteristic features of modern frogs – a broad head with large orbits for the eyes; a short spine with eight presacral vertebrae (anything from five to nine in other frogs); a single sacral vertebra (the "hump" in sitting frogs, pp. 42–43); the urostyle, a peculiar, rod-like bone formed from fused tail vertebrae; and long leg, feet, and toe bones, including two elongated ankle bones which enable the legs to fold for jumping (pp. 24–27).

Large orbit, or eye socket

Presacral, or shortened, vertebra

Transverse process (no rib)

Urostyle

Elongated ankle bone

Sacral vertebra

Adult skeletons of an American bullfrog (left) and a common frog (below)

TECHNICOLOUR INSIDES
Frogs do not normally have such colourful insides. This old anatomical preparation was dissected, then injected with red dye to show up the arteries, which carry oxygenated blood, and blue for veins which carry oxygen-depleted blood. A frog's heart has three chambers – not four as in mammals. There is a pair of lungs, and the gut is divided into five distinct regions – stomach, duodenum, small intestine, colon, and rectum. A single opening – the cloaca – is present for getting rid of waste products from the gut and urinary bladder and it is also part of the reproductive system. The paired kidneys are visible, but the ovaries, chest muscles, and bones of the pectoral girdle have been removed from this female frog.

SUCCESSFUL BLUEPRINT
The frog skeleton is the basis of a very successful amphibian body plan. With relatively few, simple modifications, some frogs have become adapted to life in trees (pp. 50–53), and even underground (pp. 54–55). This European common frog skeleton may look small, but adult frogs of other species vary from the size of a 1-cm (0.4-in) long housefly to a fully-grown, 40-cm (16-in) long chicken.

SALAMANDER-STYLE SKELETON
Of all modern amphibians, newts and salamanders have changed least from the body shapes of their ancestors (pp. 8–9). This skeleton of a juvenile Japanese giant salamander – a mere baby at 0.6 m (2 ft) – shows some characteristic features of salamanders. They have small- to medium-sized openings for the eyes, there are about 16 to 22 presacral vertebrae (with a pair of ribs on each, except the first), a sacral, and about 18 to 20 vertebrae in the tail. Also, the front and hind legs are about the same in size and length.

Sacral vertebra (wider processes, no ribs)

Tail vertebra

Compact, narrow skull

Rib

One of five toes

Left hind foot

WORM, SNAKE, OR AMPHIBIAN?
From the outside, caecilians look rather like worms (pp. 46–47); although under the skin they look more like snakes, they are true amphibians. The lack of eyes and limbs, the small, compact skull, and the increase in the number of rib-bearing vertebrae (often 100, or more, as shown here), are the results of extreme adaptation to a worm-like, burrowing way of life.

Skeleton of a caecilian

The importance of water

WATER IS AN ESSENTIAL PART of amphibian life. Fresh water keeps amphibian skin moist and is necessary for reproduction – especially in species that spend all, or part, of their lives as larvae under water. In aquatic or watery habitats, water passes rapidly through the skin and has to be eliminated via the kidneys. In dry areas amphibians risk losing more water than they can take up. Frogs can reduce water loss by having a less porous skin, by seeking out damp, shady places, by burrowing, and by taking up water from damp or wet surfaces. Some toads obtain almost three-quarters of the water they need through a baggy patch or "seat" on their pelvis which they press against moist surfaces. Amphibians rarely drink water, although a little may be taken in with their food.

In spite of their vulnerability to sudden water uptake or loss, many amphibians have adapted their behaviour and skin surface structure to a surprising variety of habitats – to life in ponds and in trees (even high in the forest canopy where the only free-standing water collects in pockets formed by leaves), and to life in the desert, by burrowing and forming cocoons.

FLOWER POWER
Thumbelina is a children's story about a tiny flower fairy stolen by a toad, who wanted Thumbelina to marry his ugly son. The old toad imprisoned Thumbelina on a lily pad in the middle of a river, but helped by the fishes, she escaped and eventually married the Prince of the Flower People.

SHIP OF THE DESERT
Contrary to popular opinion, camels do not store water in their humps (which are fat reserves), but drink large quantities of water to replace what they have lost.

Female great crested newt

WET AND DRY
Great crested newts spend most of the year on land, returning to the water to breed in spring (pp. 40–41). In the water they shed their dry, warty skin for a smoother one.

BREATHING UNDERWATER
The larva of the tiger salamander uses its three pairs of large, feathery gills to breathe underwater. The deep red gills are rich in blood vessels, which absorb the dissolved air from the water.

One of three pairs of gills

Young tiger salamander with gills

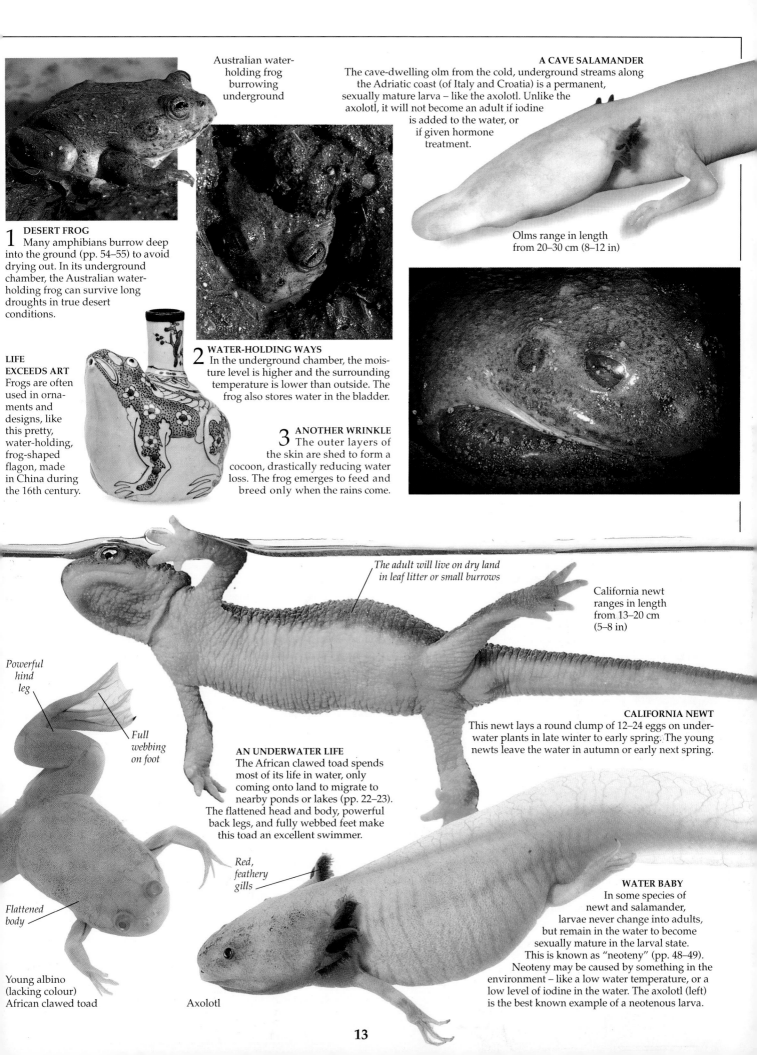

1 DESERT FROG
Many amphibians burrow deep into the ground (pp. 54–55) to avoid drying out. In its underground chamber, the Australian water-holding frog can survive long droughts in true desert conditions.

Australian water-holding frog burrowing underground

A CAVE SALAMANDER
The cave-dwelling olm from the cold, underground streams along the Adriatic coast (of Italy and Croatia) is a permanent, sexually mature larva – like the axolotl. Unlike the axolotl, it will not become an adult if iodine is added to the water, or if given hormone treatment.

Olms range in length from 20–30 cm (8–12 in)

LIFE EXCEEDS ART
Frogs are often used in ornaments and designs, like this pretty, water-holding, frog-shaped flagon, made in China during the 16th century.

2 WATER-HOLDING WAYS
In the underground chamber, the moisture level is higher and the surrounding temperature is lower than outside. The frog also stores water in the bladder.

3 ANOTHER WRINKLE
The outer layers of the skin are shed to form a cocoon, drastically reducing water loss. The frog emerges to feed and breed only when the rains come.

The adult will live on dry land in leaf litter or small burrows

California newt ranges in length from 13–20 cm (5–8 in)

Powerful hind leg

Full webbing on foot

CALIFORNIA NEWT
This newt lays a round clump of 12–24 eggs on underwater plants in late winter to early spring. The young newts leave the water in autumn or early next spring.

AN UNDERWATER LIFE
The African clawed toad spends most of its life in water, only coming onto land to migrate to nearby ponds or lakes (pp. 22–23). The flattened head and body, powerful back legs, and fully webbed feet make this toad an excellent swimmer.

Red, feathery gills

Flattened body

WATER BABY
In some species of newt and salamander, larvae never change into adults, but remain in the water to become sexually mature in the larval state. This is known as "neoteny" (pp. 48–49). Neoteny may be caused by something in the environment – like a low water temperature, or a low level of iodine in the water. The axolotl (left) is the best known example of a neotenous larva.

Young albino (lacking colour) African clawed toad

Axolotl

Colours and markings

AMPHIBIANS HAVE AN INCREDIBLE RANGE of colours and markings, from bright blues, reds, and yellows to muddy browns and greens, with a variety of stripes and spots. Many amphibians are darker on top, with a completely different colour and pattern underneath. Like most animals, amphibians either blend in with their surroundings for camouflage (pp. 20–21), or are highly coloured to show predators that they are poisonous to eat (pp. 56–57). An amphibian's colour may also help absorb or reflect heat, or attract a mate (pp. 32–35). The main colour and markings in an amphibian's skin are produced by three different colour pigment cells – white, yellow, and brown-black – which are found deep in the skin. There is no green or blue pigment – a frog looks green when the blue part of white light is absorbed by yellow cells. Brown-black pigment cells can expand to darken, or contract to lighten, the animal's skin. An amphibian's colour varies with humidity and temperature – it may become pale when warm and dry, darker if cold and damp.

THE FROG PRINCE
The story of the princess who kisses a frog, magically turning him into a handsome prince, is a well-known fairy tale. In the 1815 version by the Brothers Grimm, the princess dislikes the frog, but he tricks her into caring for him, breaking the wicked witch's spell.

White's treefrogs from Australia (above) and Indonesia (left)

THE SAME BUT DIFFERENT . . .
The intricate patterns on the upper surfaces of the head, body, arms, and legs of these two primarily green horned toads from South America give them their common name of "ornate" horned toad (pp. 44–45). The small individual differences in skin colours and markings (left and below) are common within a species.

DARKEN DOWN, LIGHTEN UP!
A change in the background colour of an amphibian is a response to changes in the strength of light, temperature, moisture, or even mood. Light green is the usual colour for these White's treefrogs (pp. 50–51), but if they move away from a leaf's sunlit surface to a cool, shady, or damp place they may change from green to light brown.

Short, sturdy leg

Enormous mouth for grabbing large prey

Pattern breaks up toad's shape

Three ornate horned toads (left) from South America, from 9–13 cm (3.5–5 in) long

DIFFERENT COLOUR, DIFFERENT SPECIES
This brown form of horned toad (left) was thought to belong to the same species as the two green ones, but it was recognized as different in 1980. Although the pattern is similar, they are found in different, but nearby, habitats and do not interbreed in the wild. They are not polymorphic forms because they are not members of the same species.

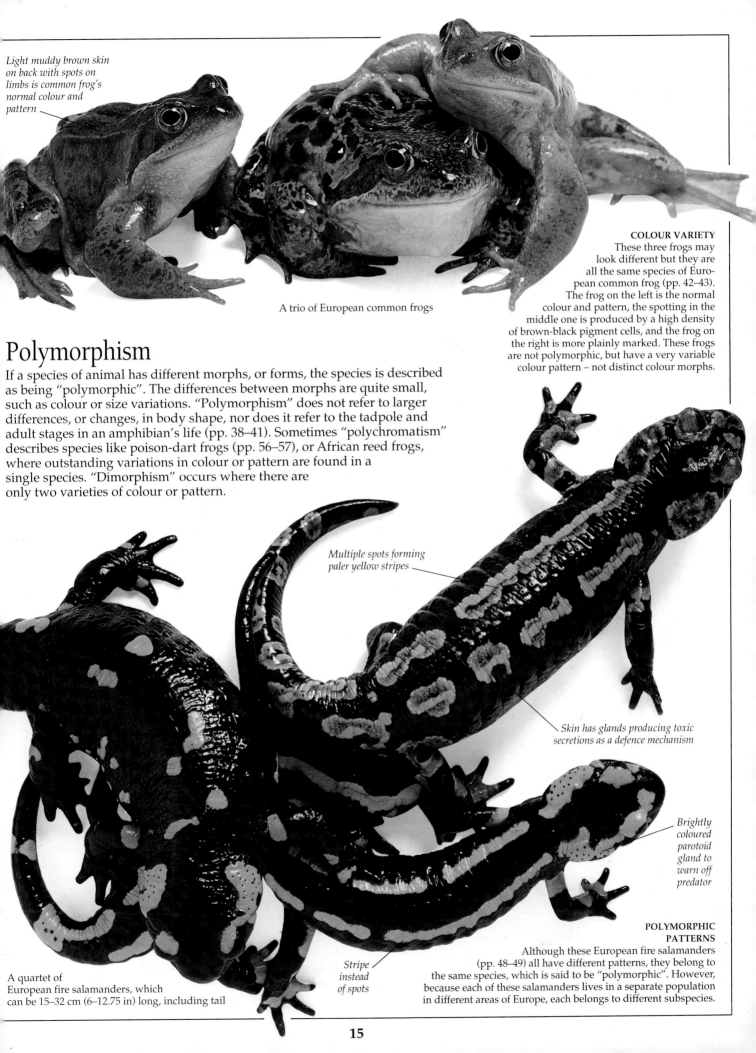

Light muddy brown skin on back with spots on limbs is common frog's normal colour and pattern

A trio of European common frogs

COLOUR VARIETY
These three frogs may look different but they are all the same species of European common frog (pp. 42–43). The frog on the left is the normal colour and pattern, the spotting in the middle one is produced by a high density of brown-black pigment cells, and the frog on the right is more plainly marked. These frogs are not polymorphic, but have a very variable colour pattern – not distinct colour morphs.

Polymorphism

If a species of animal has different morphs, or forms, the species is described as being "polymorphic". The differences between morphs are quite small, such as colour or size variations. "Polymorphism" does not refer to larger differences, or changes, in body shape, nor does it refer to the tadpole and adult stages in an amphibian's life (pp. 38–41). Sometimes "polychromatism" describes species like poison-dart frogs (pp. 56–57), or African reed frogs, where outstanding variations in colour or pattern are found in a single species. "Dimorphism" occurs where there are only two varieties of colour or pattern.

Multiple spots forming paler yellow stripes

Skin has glands producing toxic secretions as a defence mechanism

Brightly coloured parotoid gland to warn off predator

POLYMORPHIC PATTERNS
Although these European fire salamanders (pp. 48–49) all have different patterns, they belong to the same species, which is said to be "polymorphic". However, because each of these salamanders lives in a separate population in different areas of Europe, each belongs to different subspecies.

Stripe instead of spots

A quartet of European fire salamanders, which can be 15–32 cm (6–12.75 in) long, including tail

Self-defence

MOST AMPHIBIANS ARE HARMLESS but they have many enemies and each year millions are eaten by other animals. While many produce poisonous chemicals in their skin, unlike snakes, spiders, and scorpions, they lack the means of inflicting a poisonous bite or sting. An amphibian's poison-defence works only if a predator tries to eat it. The main defence is camouflage (pp. 20–21) – remaining hidden and not being seen. If disturbed, many amphibians use a startling display behaviour to frighten the enemy away or give themselves time to escape. The use of poison (pp. 56–57) is usually a last resort in a series of defence strategies used to avoid being eaten.

POISONOUS NEWT
The red eft is the land-dwelling, sub-adult stage of the eastern newt from North America. It spends two to three years on land before it returns to water as a fully adult newt. Its red colour tells predators that it is poisonous and distasteful to eat.

RED MIMIC
The bright red-coloured red salamander is a mimic – that is, it looks and behaves like the poisonous red eft of the eastern newt (above). In this case the mimic is also poisonous and benefits because predators have learned to avoid the more common newt.

HIDE OR DAZZLE
The colourful fire-bellied toads normally rely on their excellent camouflage (pp. 20–21) to stay hidden from enemies. If faced by a predator, with no chance of escape, the toad goes into a defence posture – arching its back and showing the bright, warning colours of its hands, feet, and belly.

Oriental fire-bellied toad

Yellow-bellied toad (below)

European fire-bellied toad

Parotoid, or poison, gland

POISON GLANDS
True toads, like the European green toad, have an enlarged parotoid, or poison, gland behind each eye. If a toad is threatened by a predator, a poisonous, milky secretion oozes from the gland's pores. When the gland is pressed, the toad can squirt the secretion for a short distance. If the predator gets the poison in its eyes or mouth, it suffers a burning sensation and muscle spasms, causing heartbeat and breathing difficulties.

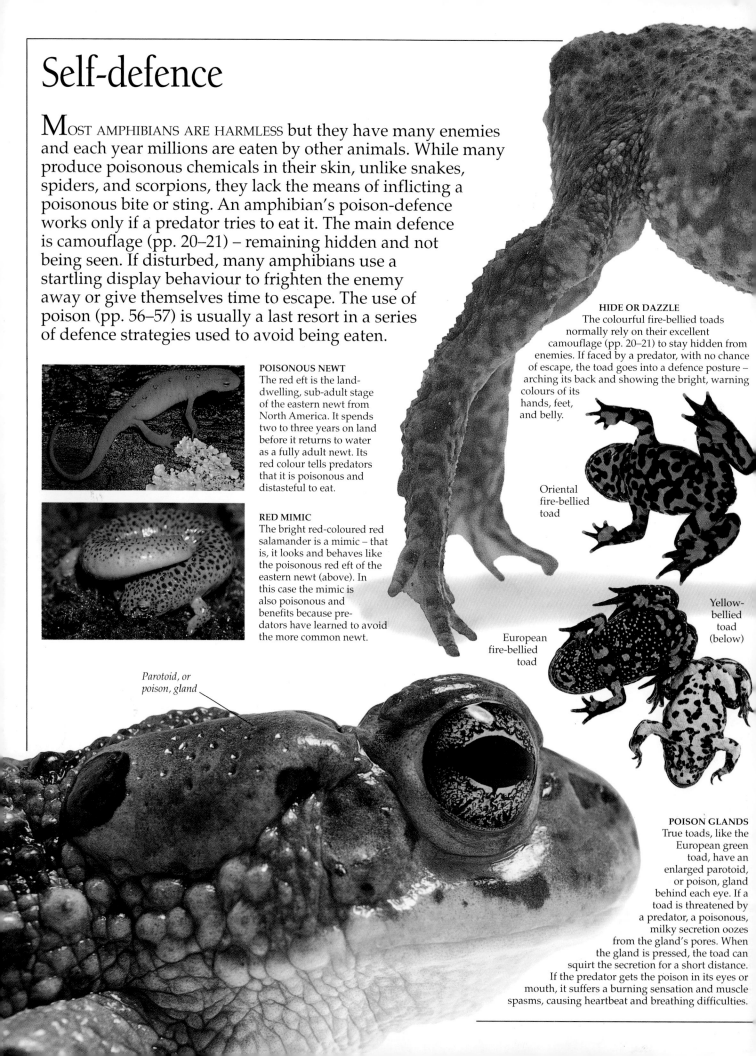

Frogs and toads often inflate their lungs with air if upset or disturbed – if threat increases they stand straight-limbed

Chilean four-eyed frog at rest

Parotoid gland

Chilean four-eyed frog when threatened

Eyespot

SUDDEN SHOCK

The Chilean four-eyed frog has a pair of glandular eyespot markings on its flanks, which are normally covered by the thighs when the frog is at rest. If the frog is threatened, it will suddenly expose the eyespots – enough to startle almost any enemy. The "eyespot surprise" bluff is backed up by a foul-tasting poison secreted from the glands.

CALL MY BLUFF

Many amphibians defend themselves by bluffing, pretending they are different from the way they really are. This European common toad is standing on its toes, its body inflated with air, and its head and body tilted forward towards the predatory grass snake. This makes the toad appear larger than it really is. With the parotoid glands as a back-up defence, this behaviour turns the toad from an apparently harmless victim into an aggressive, dangerous attacker. The snake will probably slither away, leaving the toad alone.

PRICKLY CUSTOMER

The Spanish sharp-ribbed salamander has needle-like rib tips, which can actually pass through the skin of its body wall. This teaches any would-be predator a sharp lesson.

Sharp rib tip

RAGING BULLFROG

This Budgett's frog from Argentina may look harmless, even funny (top), but an angry Budgett's frog (left) can look quite frightening. If this frog is threatened or provoked, it will open its mouth, scream, make loud, grunting noises, and may even bite its enemy.

STRANGE POSITION

The Italian spectacled salamander uses two displays to avoid its enemies. It either plays dead, or curls its tail forward to show the bright red underside of its tail (above). Many other salamander species adopt even more unusual body postures for defence. These are usually backed up by oozing foul-tasting, or poisonous, secretions from glands on the skin's surface.

Fast food

Most amphibians will eat almost any live food that they can manage to swallow or gulp down. Insects, spiders, snails, slugs, and earthworms form the main part of the diet for most adult amphibians. Larger species, like the ornate horned toad, will take larger prey, maybe even a mouse, while some species are cannibals – a case of frog eat frog. There are also specialist feeders – some smaller frogs and toads eat only ants or termites, and one species of Brazilian treefrog eats only berries. Aquatic amphibians, like the African clawed toad (pp. 22–23), tend to hang just below the water's surface, waiting for tadpoles or small fish to swim by. All amphibians will gorge themselves if food is plentiful, to enable them to survive times when food is scarce.

Frog launching itself towards prey

1 LEAP AND SNAP FEEDING
Frogs are more active feeders than toads and will not often sit and wait for their prey – "see it and seize it" is their strategy. Launching itself towards a woodlouse, this frog has to judge the distance it needs to jump and when to open its mouth with split-second accuracy.

Woodlouse

2 READY FOR PREY
As the frog leaps it opens its mouth, ready to catch the woodlouse with its long, sticky tongue. Frogs usually go after fast-moving insects, like flies, crickets, and grasshoppers. The frog only gets one chance – if it misses it will have wasted its energy. Even the slow-moving woodlouse might fall, or get knocked off its leaf, and escape, if the frog mistimes its jump.

European common frog going after prey

Eyes open

Legs and body at full stretch

A BIG MOUTHFUL...
The ornate horned toad's huge mouth, sit-and-wait feeding method, and camouflaged body markings help it take large, passing insects, mice, and other amphibians by surprise. When a horned toad opens its mouth, the whole of the front end of its body seems to open up!

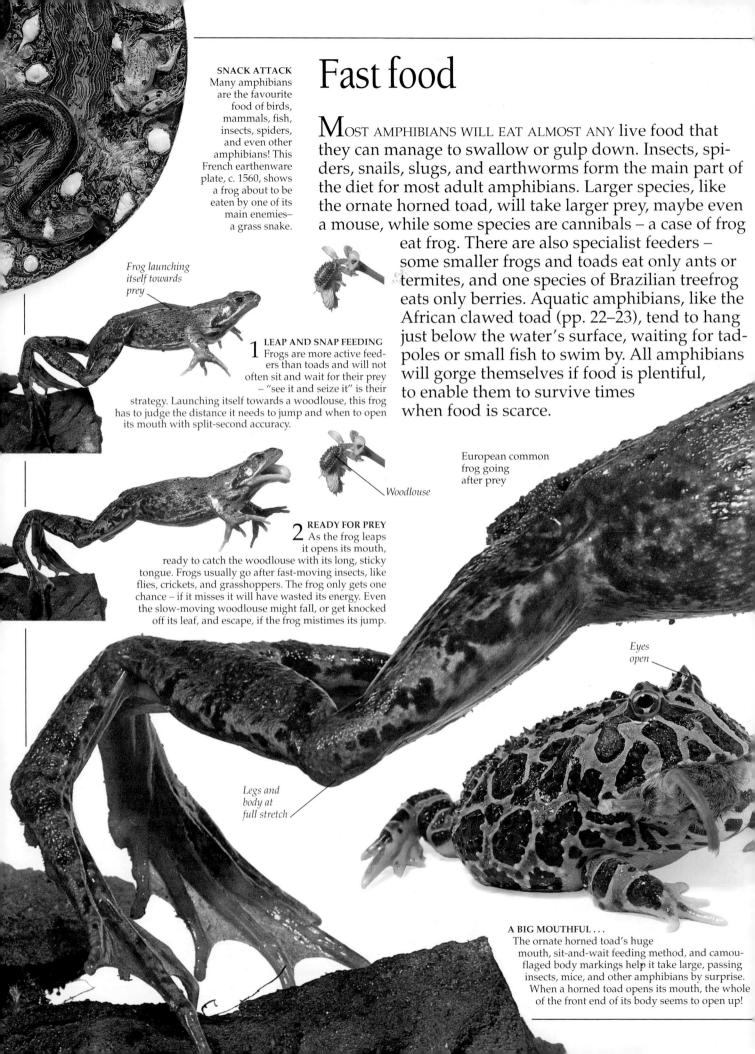

SLOW, SLOW, QUICK . . .
Newts, salamanders, and caecilians tend to eat slow-moving, soft-bodied animals, like this earthworm. They approach their prey slowly, then make a quick, last-minute grab, often turning their head on one side. They grip the food using teeth in their upper and lower jaws.

Eyelid starting to close

Woodlouse

Mandarin salamander eating an earthworm

Tongue flips out from front of mouth

3 SUCCESSFUL STRIKE
With the precision of a guided missile, homing in on its target, the frog's tongue flips out of the open mouth and strikes the woodlouse.

Making a meal of a mealworm

Watching its prey

Ready for action

TONGUE FLIPS
The boy's party whistle flips open and forward because air is blown into it, but the tongue of a frog or toad flips out and over, because muscles in the floor of the mouth push the tongue forward.

SEE IT, WATCH IT, EAT IT
Toads are careful, deliberate feeders. This common toad's attention has been attracted by a wriggling mealworm. It turns its head towards its prey, watching it intently. Some toads may even stalk their prey using creeping, cat-like movements. Suddenly, leaning over the mealworm, the toad gives a rapid tongue-flick, and the mealworm disappears. As the toad swallows it blinks and the pressure of the eyeball helps push the food down.

Tongue flicks out

Eyes firmly shut as ornate horned toad swallows its prey

. . . TAKES SOME SWALLOWING
The blinking of the eye pushes the eyeball down, increases the pressure in the mouth, and helps the toad swallow its meal.

. . . and mealworm disappears

All but the tail has disappeared

Toad swallows, blinking its eyes

Two North American treefrogs

Hide and seek

AMPHIBIANS ARE MASTERS of "camouflage" – the art of self-concealment. They have exceptional ability to use their skin colours and markings (pp. 14–15) to hide or blend in against their natural surroundings. This helps amphibians avoid being seen, either by potential prey or by predators. They can also use their skin texture. Some species have skin flaps or fringes along the edges of their bodies, which make their body outlines look like natural objects in their environment, or produce an irregular shape, which makes it even more difficult for predators to spot their prey. Remaining still or adopting a set position increases the illusion of the amphibian appearing to "melt" into the background.

HIDING IN TREES
For many species of treefrog (pp. 50–53), just being the right shade of green is camouflage enough. A light stripe on its side or yellow spots can look like sunlight on a leaf.

UNUSUAL STRATEGY
This treefrog from Brazil has a very unusual form of camouflage – it looks like a splash of bird droppings on a stone.

BREAKING UP
Many amphibians have a light line down their back or sides, breaking up the easily recognizable body shape. In some species, like this Gray's stream frog, the stripe may be quite wide.

LEAF MIMIC
This Asian horned toad provides one of the finest examples of the art of camouflage in amphibians. The body is flattened and its colour is an excellent match to the dried leaves and leaf litter on the forest floor. Skin flaps, or "horns", projecting over its eyes and on the tip of its snout look like leaf shapes, while the narrow skin ridges and glandular folds resemble leaf ribs.

PATTERN PERCEPTION
Finding an African square-marked toad against any similarly coloured background is very difficult. When the match is this good (right), and the toad remains perfectly still, it is almost impossible to see.

Asian horned toad on leaves

African square-marked toad on bark

DISAPPEARING TRICK

Away from their natural habitat, some amphibians appear far too highly coloured to ever possibly camouflage themselves safely. This Oriental fire-bellied toad looks like a toy model, painted in bright, enamel colours. Yet seen in its natural surroundings – a duckweed-covered pond, with the brighter colours submerged – this gaudy little toad is at least as difficult to see as the more subtly coloured square-marked toad.

Oriental fire-bellied toad

Spot the fire-bellied toad in duckweed

STONE FROGS

These Asian painted frogs show another aspect of camouflage coloration and behaviour. A burrowing species, this frog will dig itself into soft earth, moss, or leaf litter, with which it blends in very well. However, much of its time may be spent underground, emerging at the start of the rainy season to breed. Its smooth, wet skin and mottled colours help it to merge into a range of features – wet leaves, pebbles, and fallen trees.

Male Asian painted frog

EASILY SEEN

Against a plain background, this same African square-marked toad (left) is easily seen. All camouflaged animals have to be very careful not to move onto a background where they can be readily spotted – otherwise the advantage is instantly lost.

African square-marked toad

Female Asian painted frog is fatter and full of eggs

CLOSE MATCH

Some species may closely match details of objects in their environment or have subtleties of shading, marking, or colouring on the skin surfaces of their backs. The markings on the skin of this European yellow-bellied toad match the small, dark marks commonly found on bark, in leaf mould, or in soft earth. The small patches of colour help to disrupt the toad's shape and almost completely hide its body.

SHARED STRATEGY

Camouflage is important to the soldier and to the amphibian for the same reason – it enables both to live in a hostile world, but at the same time it provides a certain amount of personal protection.

European yellow-bellied toad on bark

European yellow-bellied toad

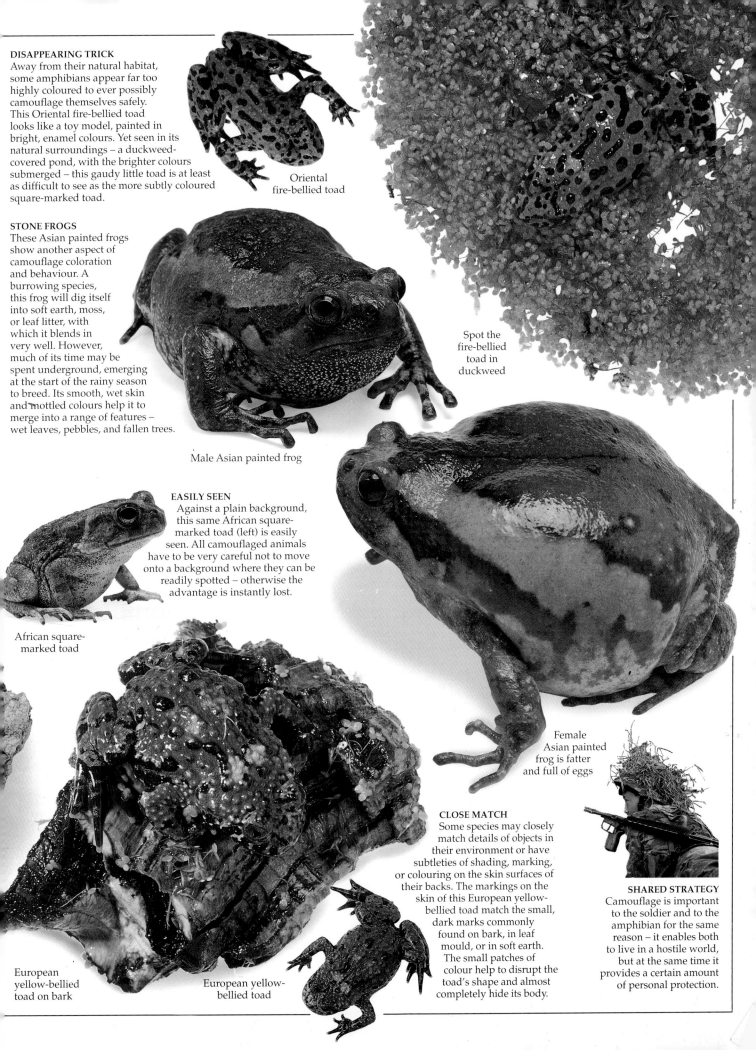

Senses and survival

NO ROAD SENSE Every year thousands of amphibians are killed on the roads on their annual migrations to and from their breeding ponds. Road signs like this (right) warn motorists about migrating frogs and toads.

LIKE OTHER ANIMALS, AMPHIBIANS HAVE five basic senses – touch, taste, sight, hearing, and smell. But they can also detect ultra-violet and infra-red light, and the Earth's magnetic field. Through touch, amphibians can feel temperature and pain, and respond to irritants, such as acids in the environment. As cold-blooded animals with porous skin, amphibians need to respond quickly to any external changes. In terrestrial (land-based) species, a sudden change in temperature can lead to death by drying out, or from freezing by rapid chilling. An amphibian's senses can also help it obtain food, find a mate, and avoid being eaten.

FEELING THE PRESSURE
Aquatic frogs have a lateral line sense system for detecting pressure changes from moving or stationary objects in the water. The individual lateral line sense organs, called plaques, are easily seen on the head and along the sides of the body on this African clawed toad.

Tentacle

MYSTERY SENSE ORGAN
Caecilians have a small tentacle emerging from the eye socket or below the eye. Its function is unknown, but it may be touch (picking up vibrations), or smell (helping to detect food, predators, or a mate).

Lateral line, or plaque

Lateral line

Eye of mandarin salamander (below)

Eye of marbled newt (below)

SIGHT AND SMELL
Terrestrial species, like the mandarin salamander (top left), need good eyesight to spot slow-moving prey in poor light, while marbled newts (below left) use sight and smell to find food. Like most newts, they react more strongly to food in water, showing that smell is more useful in an aquatic environment.

TADPOLES TOO
Lateral line systems are also found in aquatic newts, salamanders, sirens, and amphibian larvae, like this American bullfrog tadpole. Their position and development vary in different species.

DELICATE FINGERS

Surinam toads from eastern and northern parts of South America spend their entire life in water. They have long, thin, tubular fingers, which are used for catching and manipulating prey towards the mouth when feeding. The tips of the fingers are star-shaped and have eight (or 16) smooth, fine ends arranged in branched pairs. The fingers themselves are covered in tiny spines which help the adult to grip slimy prey, like fish. The star-shaped tips are only fully developed in adults, and are different in related species.

(1) Vertical pupil of red-eyed treefrog

(2) Heart-shaped pupil of Oriental fire-bellied toad

TEMPERATURE CONTROL

Amphibians rapidly lose body water by evaporation in hot or drying conditions. They can sense temperature levels and sudden dryness through the skin and control their body temperature by basking in the sun if too cold, or retreating into the shade if too hot. This painted reed frog from South Africa is reducing the area of its body surface exposed to the sun, by tucking in its front and back legs.

(3) Horizontal pupil of Asian tree toad

PERFECT PUPILS

Eye colour and pupil shape are very variable in frogs: (1) vertical, cat-like for night vision or quick response to rapidly changing light conditions; (2) heart-shaped; (3) horizontal, the more common pupil for normal daylight vision; and (4) round – newts and salamanders also have round pupils.

Ear of American bullfrog

(4) Round pupil of Madagascan tomato frog

BIG EARS

Hearing is one of the most important senses in frogs. The size of, and distance between, the ears are related to the wavelength and frequency of the sound of the male's call.

THE SWEET SMELL OF LOVE

Newts have an elaborate courtship behaviour, during which the male releases chemicals called "pheromones" from the bulbous, cloacal gland at the base of his tail. He uses his tail to waft these secretions towards the female.

Leaps and bounds

THINK OF FROGS and you imagine them jumping and leaping around. But not all frogs can leap – some walk, crawl, run, or hop for short distances, and certain tree-frogs can even "fly", or glide, from tree to tree (pp. 50–51). Almost all treefrogs have sticky, sucker-like discs, or pads, on their hands and feet for clinging onto vegetation. The way frogs move is partly related to the length of their legs – those with short legs walk, crawl, or do short hops, while long-legged frogs mostly leap or make extended hops. Their behaviour also affects the way they move – they may walk slowly, stalking their insect food, or leap away in alarm from their enemies. For any frog, the best way of escape is to hop it– to make for the nearest cover, preferably by a quick leap into water. But once in water, adult frogs swim very differently from tadpoles. Their active lifestyle and the ability to take fast-moving prey have helped make frogs and toads the most successful group of modern amphibians, in terms of variety and numbers of species (pp. 42–45).

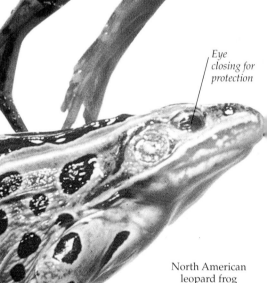

SERIOUS FUN
These children are having great fun playing leap-frog, but for real frogs leaping has a serious purpose. They leap so they can capture their food or escape from danger.

Leg stretching to full length

Eye closing for protection

Hump still visible

ONE, TWO, THREE, JUMP!
This North American leopard frog is showing how a long, graceful leap is made. When a frog is at rest on the ground, it is seated with its legs folded. Once the frog decides to leap, its specially modified heel section just above the feet (pp. 10–11), and its powerful hind leg muscles are put into action. Immediately before the leap begins, the frog tenses its leg muscles, and then presses its feet on the ground. The frog's leap has begun.

North American leopard frog prepares for take-off

Right hind leg preparing to step forward

Foot pressing down on ground

Leg muscles tensing

Front leg carried down and backwards

Male green toad (6.5 cm, 2.5 in long) starts a walk

RUN, DON'T WALK
African running frogs (pp. 44–45) live amongst hummocks, or mounds, in grassland areas – a habitat where a jumping frog might become tangled in the grass stems or leap into the path of a predator. So, walking or running with the body raised off the ground, to clear obstacles, is less dangerous.

African running frog (3 cm, 1.2 in long) in crouching position and ready for take-off

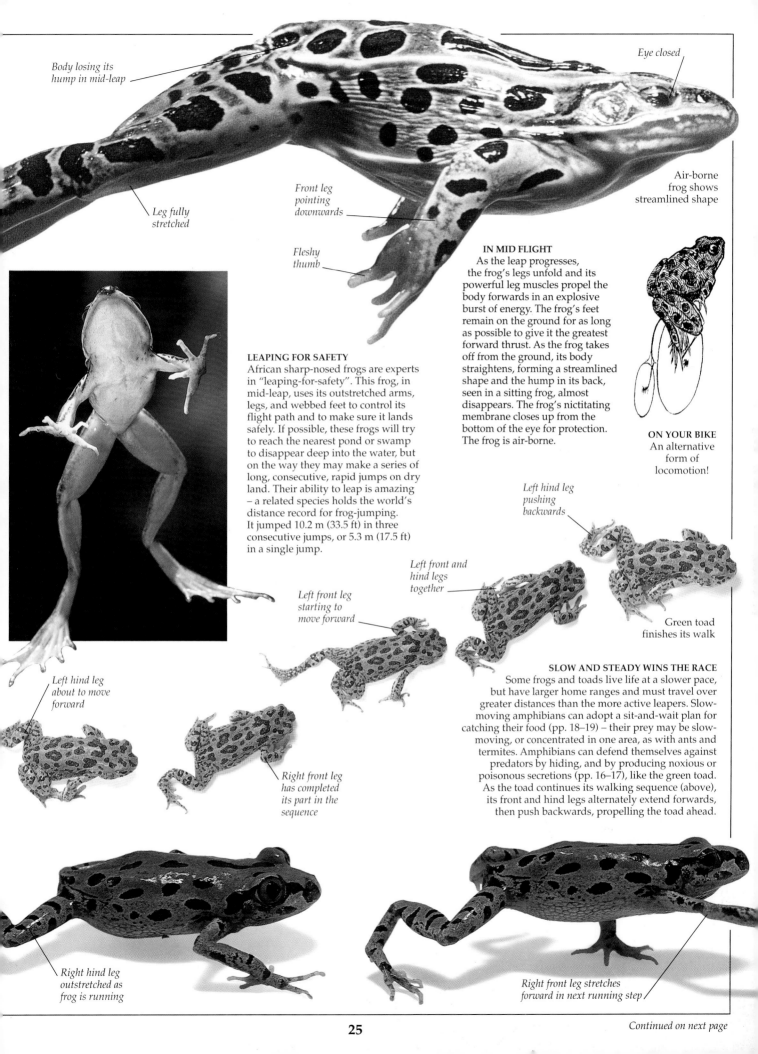

Body losing its
hump in mid-leap

Eye closed

Air-borne
frog shows
streamlined shape

Leg fully
stretched

Front leg
pointing
downwards

Fleshy
thumb

IN MID FLIGHT
As the leap progresses,
the frog's legs unfold and its
powerful leg muscles propel the
body forwards in an explosive
burst of energy. The frog's feet
remain on the ground for as long
as possible to give it the greatest
forward thrust. As the frog takes
off from the ground, its body
straightens, forming a streamlined
shape and the hump in its back,
seen in a sitting frog, almost
disappears. The frog's nictitating
membrane closes up from the
bottom of the eye for protection.
The frog is air-borne.

ON YOUR BIKE
An alternative
form of
locomotion!

LEAPING FOR SAFETY
African sharp-nosed frogs are experts
in "leaping-for-safety". This frog, in
mid-leap, uses its outstretched arms,
legs, and webbed feet to control its
flight path and to make sure it lands
safely. If possible, these frogs will try
to reach the nearest pond or swamp
to disappear deep into the water, but
on the way they may make a series of
long, consecutive, rapid jumps on dry
land. Their ability to leap is amazing
– a related species holds the world's
distance record for frog-jumping.
It jumped 10.2 m (33.5 ft) in three
consecutive jumps, or 5.3 m (17.5 ft)
in a single jump.

Left hind leg
pushing
backwards

Left front and
hind legs
together

Left front leg
starting to
move forward

Green toad
finishes its walk

Left hind leg
about to move
forward

Right front leg
has completed
its part in the
sequence

SLOW AND STEADY WINS THE RACE
Some frogs and toads live life at a slower pace,
but have larger home ranges and must travel over
greater distances than the more active leapers. Slow-
moving amphibians can adopt a sit-and-wait plan for
catching their food (pp. 18–19) – their prey may be slow-
moving, or concentrated in one area, as with ants and
termites. Amphibians can defend themselves against
predators by hiding, and by producing noxious or
poisonous secretions (pp. 16–17), like the green toad.
As the toad continues its walking sequence (above),
its front and hind legs alternately extend forwards,
then push backwards, propelling the toad ahead.

Right hind leg
outstretched as
frog is running

Right front leg stretches
forward in next running step

25

Continued on next page

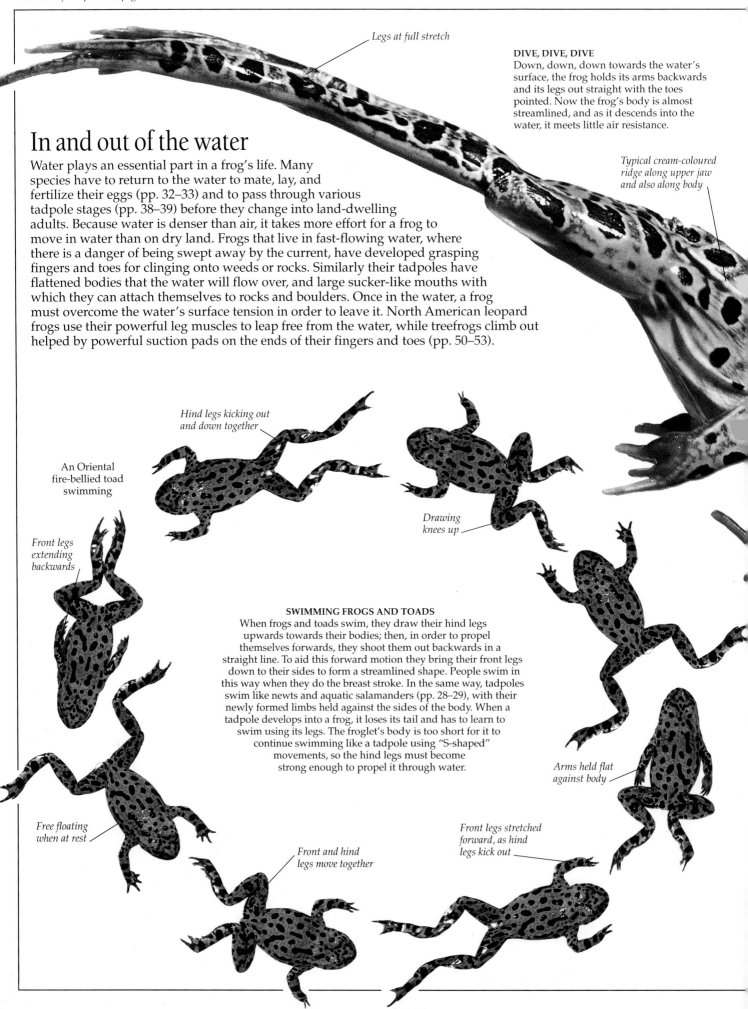

Legs at full stretch

DIVE, DIVE, DIVE
Down, down, down towards the water's surface, the frog holds its arms backwards and its legs out straight with the toes pointed. Now the frog's body is almost streamlined, and as it descends into the water, it meets little air resistance.

Typical cream-coloured ridge along upper jaw and also along body

In and out of the water

Water plays an essential part in a frog's life. Many species have to return to the water to mate, lay, and fertilize their eggs (pp. 32–33) and to pass through various tadpole stages (pp. 38–39) before they change into land-dwelling adults. Because water is denser than air, it takes more effort for a frog to move in water than on dry land. Frogs that live in fast-flowing water, where there is a danger of being swept away by the current, have developed grasping fingers and toes for clinging onto weeds or rocks. Similarly their tadpoles have flattened bodies that the water will flow over, and large sucker-like mouths with which they can attach themselves to rocks and boulders. Once in the water, a frog must overcome the water's surface tension in order to leave it. North American leopard frogs use their powerful leg muscles to leap free from the water, while treefrogs climb out helped by powerful suction pads on the ends of their fingers and toes (pp. 50–53).

Hind legs kicking out and down together

An Oriental fire-bellied toad swimming

Drawing knees up

Front legs extending backwards

SWIMMING FROGS AND TOADS
When frogs and toads swim, they draw their hind legs upwards towards their bodies; then, in order to propel themselves forwards, they shoot them out backwards in a straight line. To aid this forward motion they bring their front legs down to their sides to form a streamlined shape. People swim in this way when they do the breast stroke. In the same way, tadpoles swim like newts and aquatic salamanders (pp. 28–29), with their newly formed limbs held against the sides of the body. When a tadpole develops into a frog, it loses its tail and has to learn to swim using its legs. The froglet's body is too short for it to continue swimming like a tadpole using "S-shaped" movements, so the hind legs must become strong enough to propel it through water.

Arms held flat against body

Free floating when at rest

Front and hind legs move together

Front legs stretched forward, as hind legs kick out

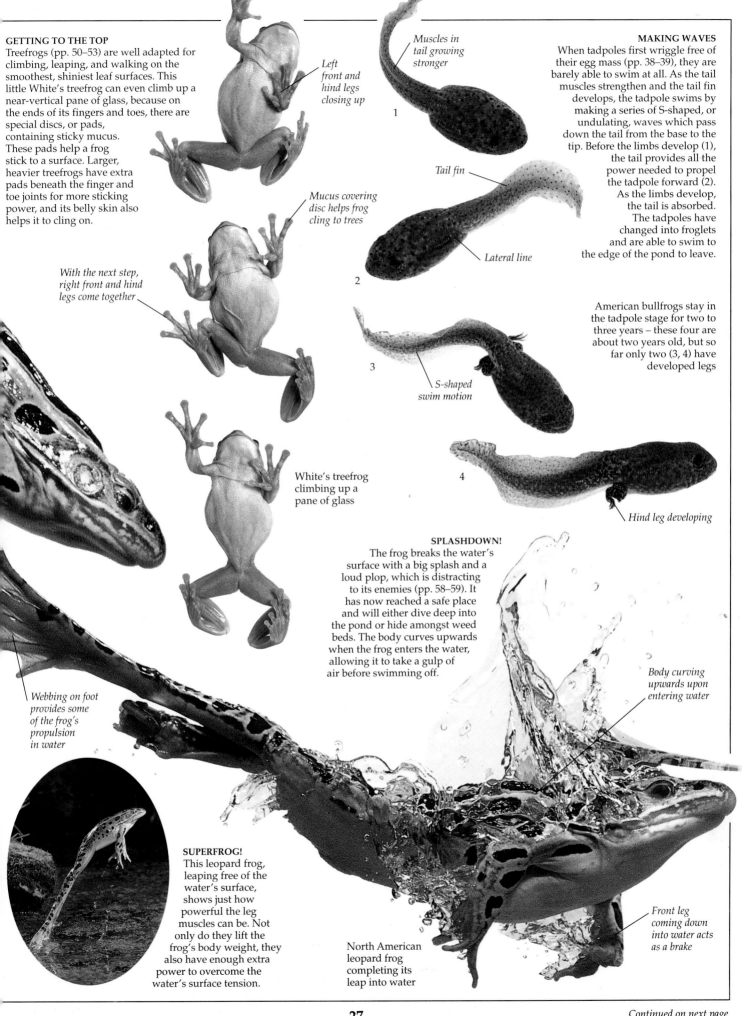

GETTING TO THE TOP

Treefrogs (pp. 50–53) are well adapted for climbing, leaping, and walking on the smoothest, shiniest leaf surfaces. This little White's treefrog can even climb up a near-vertical pane of glass, because on the ends of its fingers and toes, there are special discs, or pads, containing sticky mucus. These pads help a frog stick to a surface. Larger, heavier treefrogs have extra pads beneath the finger and toe joints for more sticking power, and its belly skin also helps it to cling on.

Left front and hind legs closing up

Mucus covering disc helps frog cling to trees

With the next step, right front and hind legs come together

White's treefrog climbing up a pane of glass

Muscles in tail growing stronger

1

Tail fin

Lateral line

2

3

S-shaped swim motion

4

MAKING WAVES

When tadpoles first wriggle free of their egg mass (pp. 38–39), they are barely able to swim at all. As the tail muscles strengthen and the tail fin develops, the tadpole swims by making a series of S-shaped, or undulating, waves which pass down the tail from the base to the tip. Before the limbs develop (1), the tail provides all the power needed to propel the tadpole forward (2). As the limbs develop, the tail is absorbed. The tadpoles have changed into froglets and are able to swim to the edge of the pond to leave.

American bullfrogs stay in the tadpole stage for two to three years – these four are about two years old, but so far only two (3, 4) have developed legs

Hind leg developing

SPLASHDOWN!

The frog breaks the water's surface with a big splash and a loud plop, which is distracting to its enemies (pp. 58–59). It has now reached a safe place and will either dive deep into the pond or hide amongst weed beds. The body curves upwards when the frog enters the water, allowing it to take a gulp of air before swimming off.

Body curving upwards upon entering water

Webbing on foot provides some of the frog's propulsion in water

SUPERFROG!

This leopard frog, leaping free of the water's surface, shows just how powerful the leg muscles can be. Not only do they lift the frog's body weight, they also have enough extra power to overcome the water's surface tension.

North American leopard frog completing its leap into water

Front leg coming down into water acts as a brake

27

Continued on next page

On all fours

Newts and salamanders (pp. 46–49) usually move quite slowly and walk or crawl – on land, underground, in the trees, or on the bottom of ponds – but they will move quickly to escape danger. Certain species can also swim and burrow: the mole and tiger salamanders which burrow with their hands and feet, and aquatic newts where the male performs a swimming courtship display in front of the female (pp. 34–35). Some salamanders, with stubby, webbed feet for gripping leaves, live among grasses, on low bushes, and even high up in the trees. So far, no "flying" salamanders have been found, but some "spring" when startled. The legless caecilians, however, must burrow – but one group has taken to the water.

Tail curving to left

SWIMMING NEWTS
Swimming involves many different leg, body, and tail movements. Newts float with their legs outstretched and body slightly inflated with air. Slow, lazy, swimming movements are made using the legs like oars in a two-person rowing boat. To move faster they paddle with the front legs alone or with the hind legs, sometimes alternately, sometimes together. Fast swimming and escape movements may also involve rapid flexing of the body and lashing the tail from side to side. Watching newts swim tells a great deal about what they are doing and how they behave.

Fire-bellied newt swimming

Foot in forward position ready for next step

Tail is straight

Foot presses against ground pushing salamander's body forward

Foot pushes body forward

Tail curves to right, helping salamander's balance

European fire salamander walking

Foot in forward position ready to press against the ground and push the animal forward

Foot moves forward

This foot pushes the body forward

1 ONWARD AND UPWARD
The European fire salamander walks slowly like most salamanders. The legs move in an alternate and opposite pattern, which means that the salamander lifts and moves the front foot of one side forward at the same time as the hind foot on the other side of its body. The other two feet remain in the same position on the ground, pushing the body forward, ready for the next step.

Foot ready to lift for next step

Foot in forward position ready to push body forward

3 FORWARD MARCH
The third step completes the sequence, with the left front and right hind feet together and the other two feet stationary. As well as pushing itself forward, this alternate and opposite walking pattern pushes the middle of the salamander's body from side to side. This swaying motion, which increases with the walking speed, looks just the same as a baby crawling.

Foot ready to lift and move forward

Foot in forward position ready to push body forward

Foot about to lift and move forward

Foot in forward position ready for next step

UNDULATING CAECILIANS
Most caecilians live in soft earth or in the leaf litter of the tropical rainforest floor. About 20 species have moved back into the water and swim using undulating, or wave-like, movements like the one above. All caecilians can burrow – the head is pushed into the soil, opening up the hole with movements of the neck. Then they either "swim" forward through the soil (using undulating movements passing back along the body), or use a special, worm-like concertina movement, where the spine (pp. 10–11) folds inside the body.

2 NEXT STEP ON
With the next step the front right and left hind feet of the salamander move together, while the other two feet stay in the same position on the ground, getting ready to push the body forward.

Foot pressing on surface, ready to push body forward

Foot about to lift

Foot ready to lift and move body forward

Foot pressing down

Foot ready to lift for next step

Foot pressing down

NEWT WALK
When on land and moving at slow speed, newts walk in a similar way to salamanders. This view from beneath shows which foot is actively pressing against the surface, pushing the newt forward, and which is being lifted off the surface before being put down again. When in water, the newt is lighter and more buoyant (just as a person is in a swimming pool) and often uses just the tips of its fingers and toes to walk over the muddy bottom of its pond.

Foot ready to lift and move body forward

View from below, showing how a newt walks

All fingers and toes

AN AMPHIBIAN'S legs, hands, and feet can give valuable clues to its habits and life-styles. A closer look at the front and back legs can reveal how an amphibian moves – whether by hopping, leaping, walking, running, crawling, digging, climbing, or even "flying" (pp. 50–51). Hands and feet also show where they live: treefrogs have discs on their fingers and toes; flying frogs have discs on their fully webbed fingers and toes; aquatic frogs and toads, as well as tree-living salamanders, have very broad, fully webbed feet; and burrowing frogs have short fingers on their hands and tubercles (projections of thickened skin) on their feet.

Large tubercle used for digging

Asian painted frog

CLIMBING HAND, BURROWING FOOT
This unusual side view of an Asian painted frog shows it is well adapted to life on the forest floor. It has large hands, with long fingers and discs on the tips for climbing, and two enlarged tubercles on each foot for burrowing (pp. 54–55).

"Extra" bone in each finger and toe

Paradoxical frog

MIXED-UP FROG
The South American paradoxical frog has a strange life history. Not only does the tadpole grow larger than the adult frog, but the adult's fingers and toes each have an extra bone, making the feet and hands very long.

Sticky disc for gripping onto leaves

White's treefrog

A GOOD CLIMBER
In most treefrogs (pp. 50–53), such as this White's treefrog from Australia, both the hands and feet are adapted to climbing. Their big hands and feet give a wide spread, so they can grip onto larger areas of leaves, twigs, and branches, and the sticky pads on their fingers and toes help them cling on.

A GREAT BURROWER
The short, stubby toes and fingers, and large, spade-like tubercles on the African bullfrog's feet are adaptations to a burrowing life (pp. 54–55). Each year it spends up to ten months underground.

African bullfrog

African clawed toad

Claw for gripping

AN UNDERWATER LIFE
The African clawed toad's narrow hands and long fingers are used to push food into the mouth. The clawed toes give a good grip on slimy surfaces and webbed feet make swimming easy in tropical African lakes.

Web for swimming

Disc forming an almost perfect circle

HOW UNUSUAL!
This treefrog from Belize may have an unusually shaped head, but it has the normal hands and feet of a treefrog (pp. 50–53), with long fingers and toes ending in sticky discs, or pads. The unusual angle at the end of each finger and toe, above each rounded disc, is produced by cartilage (a tough, elastic material), which enables the last two finger bones to slide over one another. Helped by the discs, the treefrog can prolong its contact with the surface of a tree or leaf, even if it moves a hand or foot.

Unusual head shape

Small foot with short toes

Paddle-tail newt

Fully webbed foot for swimming faster

Palmate newt

Mandarin salamander

Flattened foot for digging

FOUR FEET
These four hind feet give some idea of the variety of shape found in the feet of newts and salamanders. Some species – climbers and water dwellers that live on slippery surfaces, like paddle-tail newts – have small, fully webbed feet with very short toes, sometimes contained within the web. Male palmate newts have fully webbed feet (pp. 48–49). The mandarin and tiger salamanders have flattened, digging feet with little or no webbing.

Tiger salamander

Webbing almost non-existent

Most salamanders and newts have four fingers on their hands and five toes on their feet

Extra cartilage helps frog cling on longer to leaf

Mating embraces

F̶ROGS AND TOADS LIVE in an extraordinarily wide range of habitats, but whatever the nature of their home area – on land, in water, in trees, or underground, they have to find a suitable partner and the right conditions for egglaying (pp. 36–37). Meeting, courting, and mating are the three necessary steps before egglaying can take place. In most species, the males have a distinctive mating call which attracts females of the same species, but it may also attract predators which are always interested in large gatherings of their favourite food. Courtship behaviours help to identify the partner as a member of the same species. Amplexus – the mating embrace – places the male in the right position for fertilizing the female's eggs. Fertilization usually happens as the eggs are laid. Once a suitable spawning ground has been found, then egglaying can begin.

FROG FASTENING
Frogs and toads are popular subjects for all kinds of designs, like this 19th-century Japanese ivory netsuke, used as a kimono fastening.

SINGING AND FIGHTING
Many male frogs, like the strawberry poison-dart frogs of Central America, call and defend their territory – this is known as "lekking". The male calls from a vantage point (top) and will wrestle with any intruders (above).

TOAD HUG
Common toads often begin their mating embrace, or amplexus, out of water, the smaller male being carried to the breeding pond by the larger female. Egglaying and fertilization are delayed until they are in the water.

Male grasping female under her front legs

Male and female common toads in amplexus – on land

STUCK ON YOU
This South African rain frog is not yet "glued" onto his larger female partner – when he is, his hands will be turned palms outwards. The size difference and sticky form of amplexus prevents the male being dislodged in the underground tunnels where the female lays her eggs.

Bilobed vocal sac of male frog – sacs can also be single or paired

Frog calling underwater

THE TROUBLE WITH ADVERTISING
The huge, vocal sac of the tungara frog can inflate to about the same size as its body. A common species from Mexico, Central and South America, the tungara frog gets its name from its call – a loud "tung" whine followed by two "ara" chucks. However, for any male frog (females rarely call), advertising your presence may have its disadvantages, such as attracting predators as well as mates. Tungara frogs are sometimes eaten by certain bats (pp. 58–59), which home in on the frog's call.

Male or female tungara frogs beat up mucus and water to build a foam nest to protect and surround the egg clutch

Male

Female

Male tungara frog

A TIGHT HOLD
This male common frog is grasping his female tightly under her arms, pressing his hands against her chest – a common form of amplexus, or mating embrace. In other species, males may hold the female around the waist – in front of the back legs – or even around the head.

Nuptial pad

Male and female common frogs in amplexus – in water

THUMB PADS
Many male frogs and toads have nuptial pads – patches of roughened skin on the thumbs to help hold on to a slippery female during mating.

SLEEPING PARTNER
A female red-eyed treefrog nears a calling male. He climbs on her back, holds on, and she carries him to a spawning site.

Courtship displays

COURTSHIP AND MATING, in most newts and salamanders, involve a complex behavioural display by the male for the female. Not only does a male have to find a mate of the same species, but he has to guide the female over a small sperm packet, or spermatophore, which he deposits on the ground or in a pond. Fertilization is usually internal – the female picks up the sperm packet with her cloaca, or reproductive organ. In primitive salamanders, like a hellbender (pp. 48–49), first the female lays her eggs, over which the male deposits his sperm. Caecilians have a special kind of internal fertilization, where the male inserts the end of his cloaca into that of the female.

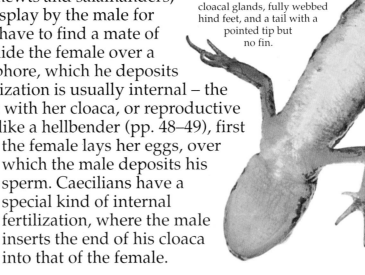

MALE PALMATE
Although he lacks the male great crested newt's dramatic, high-toothed crest, the male palmate newt is easily distinguished from the female. He has swollen cloacal glands, fully webbed hind feet, and a tail with a pointed tip but no fin.

Swollen cloacal gland

Webbed foot

Male palmate newt

1 UNDERWATER BALLET
The male great crested newt is attracted by the swollen belly of the egg-carrying female, as well as her lack of crest and silvery tail markings. She is attracted by the male's colourful nuptial, or breeding, "dress".

Female

Silvery stripe on male's tail

VAMPIRE SALAMANDER?
The male mountain dusky salamander is no vampire, but he is scraping the female's skin with his teeth to inoculate her with a chemical from his chin gland. This is to stimulate her to accept his court-ship advances.

MUSCULAR MALE
The male Spanish sharp-ribbed salamander has well-developed, muscular forearms, an adaptation for a prolonged mating embrace. Mating and egglaying can take place over ten months of the year, missing out the hottest months in Europe of July and August.

Male lashing tail towards female

2 DISPLAYING
The male swims in front of the female showing his breeding dress. Raising the toothed crest on his back, and lashing his silvery tail, he fans secretions from his cloacal glands towards the female.

Well-developed forearm for holding onto female

3 NUDGING
The male deposits his spermatophore, then guides the female over it by nudging against her side. The female uses her cloaca to pick up his sper-matophore.

FILM VAMPIRES
Hollywood vampires also use their teeth but, unlike the male salamander (top), the aim is to kill their victims.

SHOWING OFF
This 19th-century strongman shows off his strength by holding the weights with one hand, but could he hold on for 24 hours like the male sharp-ribbed salamander?

THE FEMALE OF THE SPECIES
The female palmate newt lacks the male's fully webbed hind feet, swollen cloaca, and thin tip to the tail. When she is ready to breed, her belly is full of eggs. This gives her a distinctly tubby appearance, which makes the spotting on her sides visible from underneath.

Normal tail – fin extends to tip

Thin tip to tail

No webbing on hind foot

Cloaca

Female palmate newt

Female Spanish sharp-ribbed salamander

DELICATE FEMALE
The female Spanish sharp-ribbed salamander's forearms are more slender than the male's. The male passes beneath the female and moves her onto his back. He uses his muscular forearms to hold on to her – they may stay in this position for 24 hours or more! He deposits a spermatophore which she picks up with her cloaca. Then she attaches the eggs to aquatic plants.

STRONG SALAMANDER
The male Spanish sharp-ribbed salamander is either very strong or must have fatigue-free muscles to be able to keep holding on to the female for such a long time.

Pair of mating Spanish sharp-ribbed salamanders (female above, male below)

Male Spanish sharp-ribbed salamander

Egglaying and parental care

Not all amphibians lay large numbers of eggs in water, leaving them to hatch into free-living tadpoles, like the European common frog. Many amphibians are caring parents and show more ways of caring for their eggs and young than fish, reptiles, mammals, or birds. The amount of parental care taken seems to be related to the number and size of eggs produced – fewer, larger eggs: more care; many, small eggs: less care. The kind of care taken ranges from choosing a sheltered egglaying site, to enclosing eggs in a protective foam, and egg guarding. Some amphibians carry their eggs or tadpoles on their back, or in a skin pocket; others take their eggs inside the body, into vocal sacs, or even into the stomach. There are also two species of toad, some salamanders and caecilians which give birth to live young that are tiny versions of their parents.

STOMACH UPSET
This fairy tale character looks as though she is having a bad time. So are the most remarkable frogs of all – the Australian gastric brooding frogs. First discovered in 1972, they have not been seen since 1981 and may be extinct. They were the only animals in the world known to brood their young in the female's stomach.

SAFETY DEPOSIT BOX
The back of this female marsupial, or pouched, frog from South America looks swollen. The male has placed a hundred or more fertilized eggs in the brood pouch on her back. After a period of incubation, the female makes her way to the water. Using the toes on her back feet, she then opens up the pouch, releasing the tadpoles into the water to complete their development.

EGG MIMIC
The pattern on the backs of these two glass frogs from the rainforests of Costa Rica, looks very similar to the eggs they are guarding. The male's camouflage enables them to guard their eggs in safety for 24 hours a day. As these frogs are so well camouflaged, they can avoid predators and feed on any insects that may alight on the leaf.

A LONG WAIT
This little lungless salamander, found in Costa Rica and Panama, is a devoted parent, guarding her egg clutch for some four to five months. The guarding parent, which may be either the male or the female, lies curled around the eggs which it turns occasionally. This protects the eggs from both predators and fungal infection.

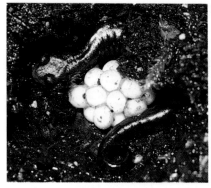

Male midwife toad, ranging from 3–5 cm (1.25–2 in) in length, carries a string of eggs

A SAFE PLACE

The female Surinam toad looks like dead leaves on the muddy bottom of the sluggish waters in South America where it lives. After mating, the male fertilizes the eggs released by the female, which stick onto a thick, spongy layer of skin on her back.

Skin of female Surinam toad swells up, almost completely covering her eggs

Some males take on two, or even three, egg clutches

POCKETS FULL OF TOADLETS

The eggs are placed on the female Surinam toad's back, when the male and female perform an egglaying roll, or loop movement, underwater. The pair are upside down when the female lays about five eggs which are fertilized and drop onto her back as the pair turn right way up in the water. In all, about 55 eggs are laid in this way. After four weeks they hatch as perfect, small toadlets.

HITCHING A LIFT

This little, non-poisonous frog from Trinidad is related to the more brightly coloured poison-dart frogs (pp. 56–57) from Central and South America. In this species, the male stays with its egg clutch. When they hatch, he carries the entire tadpole brood on his back to a nearby stream to complete their development. In other closely related species, the female is the tadpole carrier.

VOCAL SAC BROODING

The male Darwin's frog from Chile watches over his developing clutch of eggs and when the newly hatched tadpoles start to squirm, he takes them into his vocal sac. The tadpoles remain there, apparently receiving some form of nourishment, until they are ejected as tiny froglets.

THE MALE MIDWIFE

The male midwife toad from western Europe shows a unique form of parental care – he carries his eggstring of some 35–50 eggs, wrapped around his hind legs. After the eggs are laid and fertilized, he keeps hold of the female and, moving his legs alternately back and forth through the eggs, fastens them securely around his legs. After about three weeks, he takes his egg load into the water where the tadpoles hatch and complete their development.

Very short tail

NOW A FROGLET
At 12 weeks, the tail has reduced to a bud and will soon disappear. The froglets are ready to leave the water. Every generation re-enacts the transition from water to land that occurred in the first amphibians (pp. 8–9).

Metamorphosis

METAMORPHOSIS IS the change from the larval, or tadpole, stage into an adult. Amphibians are the only four-limbed, or land, vertebrates (animals with a backbone) to develop in this way, which is easier to see in frogs and toads than in other amphibians (pp. 40–41). Frog and toad larvae, or tadpoles, look completely different from their parents. The most notable difference is that a tadpole has an all-in-one head and body, as well as a long tail. At first a tadpole lacks legs, which develop later, and it must live in water to survive. The time taken to develop from eggs hatching to a fully-formed froglet varies from about 12 to 16 weeks, but this time span is greatly affected by water temperature and food supply. Tadpoles found in colder regions, at high altitudes, or from spawn laid in the breeding season, may hibernate in the tadpole state, and will not turn into a frog until the following spring. Not all frogs and toads have a free-living tadpole. For some, development takes place within an egg or inside the body of a parent (pp. 36–37).

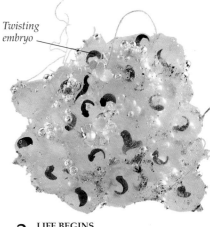

Twisting embryo

2 LIFE BEGINS
The first signs of life are when the central yolk divides in two, then four, and then eight – until it looks like a berry inside a jelly coating. The developing embryo, or tadpole, grows longer and twitching, pre-hatching movements may be seen. Hatching will take place about six days after fertilization.

Frog's egg

Female common frog

A pair of common frogs in amplexus

Male common frog

1 A TIGHT SQUEEZE
The male frog is clasping the female underneath him, in a tight mating embrace, called "amplexus". The male's arms grasp the female behind her front legs, as shown here – in other species, the grasp may be in front of her hind legs or around her head. Amplexus can last for several days. The male fertilizes the eggs – the numbers can vary from a single one up to 20,000, or more – as they are laid. They may be laid singly, in clumps, or in strings (pp. 36–37).

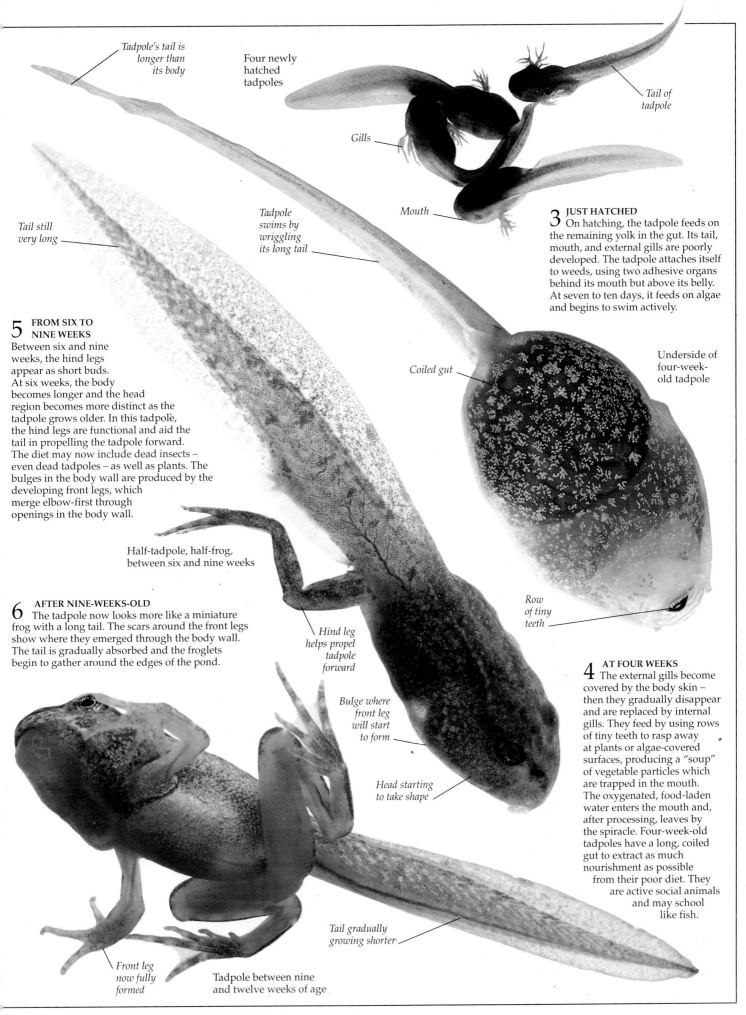

Tadpole's tail is
longer than
its body

Four newly
hatched
tadpoles

Tail of
tadpole

Gills

Mouth

3 JUST HATCHED
On hatching, the tadpole feeds on
the remaining yolk in the gut. Its tail,
mouth, and external gills are poorly
developed. The tadpole attaches itself
to weeds, using two adhesive organs
behind its mouth but above its belly.
At seven to ten days, it feeds on algae
and begins to swim actively.

Tail still
very long

Tadpole
swims by
wriggling
its long tail

Coiled gut

Underside of
four-week-
old tadpole

**5 FROM SIX TO
NINE WEEKS**
Between six and nine
weeks, the hind legs
appear as short buds.
At six weeks, the body
becomes longer and the head
region becomes more distinct as the
tadpole grows older. In this tadpole,
the hind legs are functional and aid the
tail in propelling the tadpole forward.
The diet may now include dead insects –
even dead tadpoles – as well as plants. The
bulges in the body wall are produced by the
developing front legs, which
merge elbow-first through
openings in the body wall.

Half-tadpole, half-frog,
between six and nine weeks

Row
of tiny
teeth

6 AFTER NINE-WEEKS-OLD
The tadpole now looks more like a miniature
frog with a long tail. The scars around the front legs
show where they emerged through the body wall.
The tail is gradually absorbed and the froglets
begin to gather around the edges of the pond.

Hind leg
helps propel
tadpole
forward

Bulge where
front leg
will start
to form

Head starting
to take shape

4 AT FOUR WEEKS
The external gills become
covered by the body skin –
then they gradually disappear
and are replaced by internal
gills. They feed by using rows
of tiny teeth to rasp away
at plants or algae-covered
surfaces, producing a "soup"
of vegetable particles which
are trapped in the mouth.
The oxygenated, food-laden
water enters the mouth and,
after processing, leaves by
the spiracle. Four-week-old
tadpoles have a long, coiled
gut to extract as much
nourishment as possible
from their poor diet. They
are active social animals
and may school
like fish.

Tail gradually
growing shorter

Front leg
now fully
formed

Tadpole between nine
and twelve weeks of age

Early days

LIKE FROGS AND TOADS, newts, salamanders, and caecilians undergo a metamorphosis, or period of larval development, but the change in their body shape is less marked. In newts and salamanders, the larva looks more like the adult. The development of the great crested newt is typical of species with aquatic larvae, but many salamanders do not have a free-living larval stage. Instead the female salamander may lay her eggs on land to be guarded by either parent, or may retain the eggs in her body (pp. 36–37). In each case, the salamander's egg and larval development is the same as that of the newt, but takes place inside either the egg capsule or the female's body. In caecilians, the species with free-living larvae have large gills and, like the adults, are limbless.

Developing embryo

Female great crested newt

Egg, previously wrapped in leaf that has opened, will become part of food chain

Female uses her feet to wrap newly laid egg in leaf of waterweed

Newly laid egg

EGG SANDWICH
Newts lay their eggs singly. The female wraps a waterweed leaf around each egg immediately after laying to hide it from predators, and so it has a greater chance of hatching. This leaf has opened, exposing the white egg, which probably will be eaten by a passing fish.

1 CAREFUL MOTHERS
This female newt is using her feet to wrap waterweed carefully around every egg she lays. Eggwrapping is a simple way of protecting them (pp. 36–37) and is much better than leaving them exposed in open water. Females of some other newts (pp. 46–49) – such as those of eastern North America and the fire-bellied newts of the Far East – show this egg-wrapping habit. They lay between 200 and 400 eggs in this way.

40

2 EARLY DAYS FOR A NEWT EMBRYO
At first, the egg divides like a frog's egg – into two, then four, then eight cells, and so on, until a berry-like cluster of cells is produced. After a week or so an embryo, with a recognizable head, tail, and limb buds, is formed (left). Development is rapid and the egg hatches after only about three weeks.

Feathery gill

Newt larva

Internal organs and gut visible through transparent skin

One of three pairs of feathery gills

3 NEWLY HATCHED TO EIGHT WEEKS
Newt larvae have large eyes and usually feed on water fleas and bloodworms. They have three pairs of feathery gills, unlike frog tadpoles which have only two (pp. 38–39). Newt larvae also develop their front legs first, but frog tadpoles get their hind legs first.

Typical large eye

Eight-week-old newt larva

Smaller back leg

Long, spindly front leg

4 EIGHT WEEKS AND AFTER
The body lengthens, the tail grows stronger, and the body outline begins to take shape. The back legs are much smaller than the long, spindly front legs. As development continues, the larva's head, mouth, body, legs, and tail take on a more adult shape. Some amphibians, such as axolotls (pp. 12–13), never develop beyond the larval stage.

Young tiger salamander with few gills remaining

Remains of gills

Young tiger salamander's tail is almost same length as its body

Feathery gill

Young tiger salamander with full gills

YOUNG TIGERS
Tiger salamander larvae are large – 1.25 cm (0.5 in) long when they hatch and 10 cm (4 in) when they develop into young adults 12 weeks later. These two young tigers show the change from a gilled larva (left) to a nearly-transformed young with tiny gill remnants (above). A young salamander will eat almost any food it can get into its mouth (pp. 18–19), a habit which continues during its life. This is why it is so large – up to 4 cm (1.5 in) longer than a Pacific giant salamander.

Frog or toad?

FROGS AND TOADS are the most easily recognized amphibians, because they have such a distinctive body shape. Separating this group into "frogs" and "toads" is not so easy, as the features used to distinguish between them do not apply in all cases. In general, frogs are more active, are found in or near water, have smooth skins, long hind legs, and fully webbed feet, while toads tend to be less active, prefer to live on land, have dry, warty skins, and little or no webbing. Yet some frogs do not live near water and have little or no webbing on their feet, and some toads have a smooth skin. The word "frogs" is often used by experts, to include both frogs and toads.

Smooth skin not typical in toads

Disc on finger

Slender body

TREE TOAD
This Asian tree toad is quite frog-like – it has a smoother skin than most other toads and has discs on its fingers – like the banana treefrog (bottom right). However, it belongs to the same family as the common toad (top right).

TRUE FROG
The European common frog is a typical, or true, frog – it has a smooth, wet skin, slender body, long back legs, and webbed feet used for swimming. Some frogs stay in the water, while others leave for damp, grassy areas and are rarely seen outside the breeding season, which is how they got the Latin name of *Rana temporaria*, meaning "temporary frog". *Rana* is found throughout the world, except in polar regions, but there is only one species in Australia.

Illustration by
Sir John Tenniel
(1820–1914)

ALICE AND THE FROG
In *Through the Looking Glass*, English writer Lewis Carroll (1832–1898) created the character of Alice, who on her adventures meets and befriends a frog.

Long hind leg

Typical smooth, wet skin of frog

Webbing on foot

European common frog

Long leg

Smooth, wet skin

Dry, warty skin

Short leg

Frog

Toad

LOOKING FOR DIFFERENCES
The difference between the long (jumping) legs of frogs and the short (walking) legs of toads is clearly seen above, but some species of frog have short legs. Biologists have tried to find other ways of telling frogs and toads apart and were hopeful when they discovered two chest carti- lages that were joined together in frogs and overlapping in toads. But in Darwin's frog these cartilages are partly joined and partly overlapping.

Parotoid gland

TRUE TOAD
The European common toad is a typical toad – it has a dry, warty skin, poison, or parotoid, glands behind the eyes, a squat, or tubby, body, short legs for walking or hopping, and less webbing on its feet than frogs have. Toads prefer dry land, but enter water in the breeding season – others hibernate, or overwinter, in water.

Squat body

Dry, warty skin

European common toad

Almost no webbing on foot

Short leg

Lateral line

TREEFROG?
This little treefrog has overlapping chest cartilages – which normally would make it a toad – yet it has a smooth skin and a frog-like appearance.

AFRICAN CLAWED FROG . . . OR TOAD?
Some people call this a clawed frog, and others a clawed toad. It has a very smooth skin, lives in water, and has fused chest cartilages, so it should be called a frog. However, scientific names are less confusing – it is known as a *Xenopus* (zen-o-puss) throughout the world.

Banana treefrog

Continued on next page

Loads of toads and frogs

There are more than 3,500 species of frog, but new species are still being discovered every year (pp. 60–61). Frogs are by far the largest and most successful group of modern amphibians and are found in all the world's continents, except Antarctica. Although a few species are adapted to living in cold conditions and others live in deserts, the greatest variety is found living in tropical rainforests. Frogs have a wide range of lifestyles – aquatic, terrestrial, and arboreal – that is, they live in water, on land, and in trees, respectively. Some frogs are totally aquatic, like the African clawed toad (pp. 22–23), while semi-terrestrial species live in and around ponds, lakes, fast-flowing rivers, and torrential streams. Wholly terrestrial species include burrowing frogs, like the mole frog, which cannot swim in water. The arboreal, or tree-, frogs are also found in bushes, on sedges and grasses, as well as in trees. Frogs have evolved a wide range of body shapes, sizes, and colours, that enable them to survive in widely diverse habitats.

AUSTRALIAN BURROWER
Many frogs and toads burrow (pp. 54–55), but the aptly named mole frog from Western Australia is a supreme example of adapting to life underground. A "head-first" burrower with a small head and tiny eyes, it uses its powerful, muscular front legs, broad hands, and stubby fingers to dig, in a mole-like fashion. It lives on termites and only comes to the surface to mate – when it rains.

EUROPEAN GREEN
Most treefrogs (pp. 50–53) live in South America, but this pretty little green treefrog, at 4–6 cm (1.5–2.5 in) in length, is common in most of Europe, into Africa and Asia. It lives in woods and scrubland, and only leaves its tree-top life to mate in ponds during the spring.

Typical brightly-coloured foot

Warty, toad-like skin

AFRICAN GIANT
Adult African bullfrogs can grow to 20 cm (8 in) in length. The males can be very aggressive when defending their territories against intruders – human or even other bullfrogs – and are capable of inflicting a nasty bite (pp. 18–19).

Related species can have much smaller, or no, horns

At 18.5 cm (7.5 in) long the African bullfrog is large, but the Goliath frog from West Africa is the world's biggest frog – up to 40 cm (15.5 in) long

A HORNED TOAD FROM ASIA
The fleshy horns projecting over the eyes and beyond the snout make this a very effective leaf-lookalike (pp. 20–21).

ASIAN ARBOREALS
The Asian tree toad, at 5–10 cm (2–4 in) long, is an unusual toad with discs on its fingers and toes. Good climbers, they live in trees and bushes near streams in the forests of Thailand, Sumatra, and Borneo (pp. 42–43).

Madagascan tomato frogs, from 5–7 cm (2–2.75 in) long

NO ADDED COLOURS
These four, fat tomato frogs (pp. 60–61) from northwestern Madagascar really are this deep tomato-red colour, and are shaped like a tomato as well.

African
running
frog

AFRICAN RUNNER
This brightly-coloured
frog is well camouflaged
in its natural grassland
habitat, and runs
rather than hops
(pp. 24–25).

FRIENDLY FROG
The Asian painted frog from China, Indonesia,
and India, is an attractive species. This pattern
helps it blend in with stones and rocks, which it
hides under during the day (pp. 20–21). It is often
found in parks and gardens near where humans live.

*Smaller
male*

*Bold
markings
on top side of
female's body*

A DEADLY WAITING GAME
The ornate horned toad from South America
spends most of its time half buried in forest leaf
litter or amongst moss, with just the head and eyes
showing. They are "sit-and-wait" feeders and will
grab any passing prey – large insects, other frogs,
and even small mammals (pp. 18–19).

UNINVITED GUESTS
White's treefrogs from
Australia (pp. 50–51) have an even closer
relationship with humans than the
Asian painted frogs – they are
commonly found in outside
letter boxes, in bath-
rooms, and even
in cisterns of
toilets!

*Almost actual size,
t 3 cm (1.2 in)
ong*

HIGH ALTITUDE LIVING
The Chilean red-spotted toad, found at
heights of 4000 m (13,000 ft) in
the Andes Mountains, has
had to adapt to living at
high altitudes.

IRE FROG
he West African fire
rog's skin is smooth
nd rubbery, but
oxic secretions will
oze out, if the frog is
isturbed (pp. 16–17).

Only 2.5 cm (1 in) long

45

Tailed amphibians

SALAMANDERS, NEWTS, AND SIRENS make up a group of around 360 species of tailed amphibians. Most newts and salamanders are found in the cooler, temperate, forested areas of the northern hemisphere, but one group of lungless salamanders (pp. 48–49) extends its range southwards to South America to include the high-altitude tropical cloud forests of Ecuador. Like frogs and toads, tailed amphibians have adopted a wide range of lifestyles. Some live on land in damp areas, although they may go into the water to breed (pp. 34–35). Some lungless salamanders even live in trees and have broad, flat, fully webbed hands and feet with no obvious fingers and toes. Others, like the olm and axolotl, spend their whole lives in water (pp. 12–13). The caecilians, around 170 species, are found only in the tropics and burrow in soft earth or mud, often near water, or else swim in rivers and streams.

HERALDIC SALAMANDER
This dragon-like salamander – a fabulous beast of heraldry and mythology – was the emblem of the French royal family in the early 1500s. In this detail from the painting, *The Field of the Cloth of Gold*, a salamander looks down on the meeting between England's Henry VIII and France's François I.

Short hind leg – toes more equal in size than in frogs

Tip of crest on great crested newt's tail only grows on male during mating season

Colours and patterns of tiger salamanders can vary greatly

Silvery stripe in tail of male

ON FIRE!
The sight of bright yellow and black salamanders fleeing from piles of burning logs gave rise to the belief that they lived in fire, hence their name – fire salamanders.

Tiger salamander

Well-developed tail

CAECILIANS – THE UNKNOWN AMPHIBIANS
Few biologists have seen a live caecilian and many do not realize that this group of limbless amphibians (pp. 6–7) even exists. Caecilians vary greatly in size, from 8 cm (3 in) to 1.5 m (5 ft) in length, and have either a very short tail or none at all. Females produce live young, or guard small clutches of 30 to 60 large eggs, which hatch into adult-like, gilled larvae.

Longer body than
frogs and toads

Skin folds (costal
grooves) – useful
when identifying
salamanders

SHY SALAMANDER

The term "salamander"
is generally used to refer
only to terrestrial, or land-based,
amphibians with tails, although aquatic
newts and sirens are also members of this
family. Land-dwelling salamanders are shy
creatures, living mostly in damp areas under cover
of fallen trees, logs, and rocks. They vary in size from
the tiny, dwarf Mexican lungless salamander, about
2.54 cm (1 in) long including the tail, up to this
North American tiger salamander which
can grow as long as 40 cm (15.5 in).

Front legs
only present

One of four
toes on
front foot

One of five toes
on hind foot

SALAMANDER OR SIREN?

Sirens from North America (pp. 10–11) are distinct
from salamanders in that they have lungs as well
as gills and are permanent aquatic larvae – that
is, they never develop beyond the larval
stage so never leave the water.

Lesser siren

Belly marking like a fingerprint
– every newt has a unique
set of spots

Cloacal gland,
at base of
male's tail

WATERY NEWTS

Newts are semi-aquatic
salamanders, which
return to the water in the
breeding season. They are
found in North America,
Europe, western and eastern
Asia, and Japan. The males,
particularly those of European
species like this great crested newt
(right), develop a courtship "dress" in
spring and make an elaborate display to
the female (pp. 34–35). The female lacks
the crest and silvery tail stripe of the male.

Male great crested
newt, viewed from
underneath

Continued on next page

Newt and salamander assortment

Newts and salamanders belong to a smaller group of amphibians than frogs and toads and number around 360 species. Most live in cool, temperate areas of Europe, North America, China, and Japan, but one group lives in tropical parts of South America. Adapted to a variety of habitats, they climb trees and shrubs, burrow, and lead a totally aquatic existence (pp. 28–29). The largest group, about 150 species, have lost their lungs entirely and breathe through their skin and throat instead.

"EYE OF NEWT"
The three witches in Shakespeare's *Macbeth* thought this was a necessity in their brew. "Newt" comes from the Anglo-Saxon "efete", while "an ewt" became "a newt" in Middle English. Young newts are called efts in America.

European fire salamander

SLOW MOVER
European fire salamanders are stocky and heavily built. They prefer damp areas near water and hunt slow-moving prey, such as earthworms, at night.

NEWTS GALORE
Most newts live on land, returning to the water to breed. In the breeding season, the brightly coloured male develops a crest along his back and tail. Some species also have toe webs, or fringes, which are used in courtship displays to attract the female (pp. 34–35).

The great crested newt is a protected species in the United Kingdom, but it is also found in other parts of Europe

Fire-bellied newts are found in China and Japan

Palmate newts live in Western Europe and are more aquatic than common newts

The crest of a male Italian crested newt is larger and more distinctive than in a great crested newt

The alpine newt (left) is a very pretty European species, but is not confined to alpine regions

The marbled newt from France and Spain (left) may interbreed with the great crested (above right) to produce hybrids

Broad head

Tiger salamander

Orange colour of bony crests on head and back extends full length of tail

HEAVYWEIGHT LEAGUE
The tiger salamander lives practically everywhere from arid plains to wet meadows all over North America. It is the largest living land salamander and may reach 40 cm (15.5 in) in length. They are voracious feeders and will even eat other amphibians. Like other members of the mole-salamander family, they live in burrows which either belong to other animals or which they dig for themselves.

BIG BABY
This tiger salamander larva will change into an adult when it is about 12 cm (5 in) long – unlike its relative, the axolotl, which remains in the larval state and breeds in the larval state (pp. 12–13).

Wart

ORIENTAL SALAMANDER
The mandarin salamander – or crocodile newt – is found throughout India and eastern Asia. It belongs to the same family as the newts and the fire salamander.

Flat, V-shaped head

Tiger salamander larva

Gill

Mandarin salamander

COMPETELY LUNGLESS
This dwarf Mexican lungless salamander is one of the smallest salamanders in the world, measuring less than 2.5 cm (1 in) in total length.

MOUNTAIN DWELLER
The mountain dusky salamander, from the northeastern USA, is another lungless salamander. Up to 11 cm (4.5 in) long, they are found in cool, moist areas near streams and in forests.

MUDPUPPY
The North American mudpuppy is a permanent neotenic larval species which may take up to six years to reach sexual maturity. Mud-puppies have large, deep red gills, four toes on each foot, and are related to the European olm (pp. 12–13).

Mudpuppy viewed from underneath

Gill

HELLBENDERS
These strange looking salamanders live in central-eastern USA and may grow to 75 cm (30 in) long. They are totally aquatic, living in fast-flowing streams and rivers, and are related to the Chinese and Japanese giant salamanders (pp. 10–11).

Hellbender

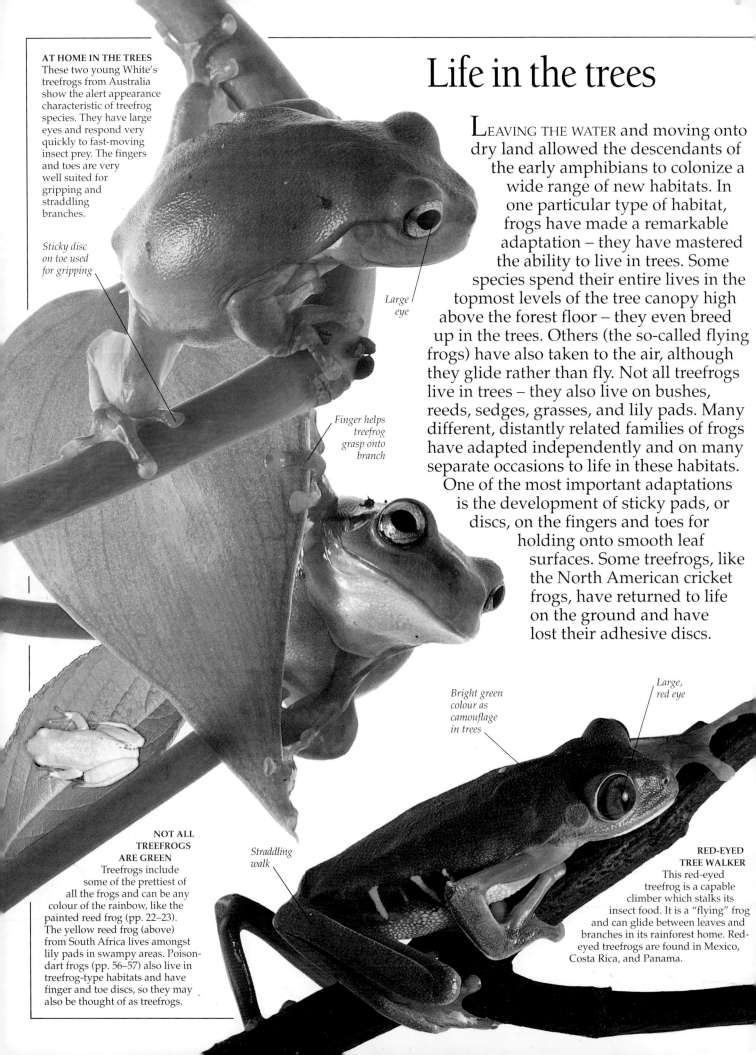

Life in the trees

LEAVING THE WATER and moving onto dry land allowed the descendants of the early amphibians to colonize a wide range of new habitats. In one particular type of habitat, frogs have made a remarkable adaptation – they have mastered the ability to live in trees. Some species spend their entire lives in the topmost levels of the tree canopy high above the forest floor – they even breed up in the trees. Others (the so-called flying frogs) have also taken to the air, although they glide rather than fly. Not all treefrogs live in trees – they also live on bushes, reeds, sedges, grasses, and lily pads. Many different, distantly related families of frogs have adapted independently and on many separate occasions to life in these habitats. One of the most important adaptations is the development of sticky pads, or discs, on the fingers and toes for holding onto smooth leaf surfaces. Some treefrogs, like the North American cricket frogs, have returned to life on the ground and have lost their adhesive discs.

AT HOME IN THE TREES
These two young White's treefrogs from Australia show the alert appearance characteristic of treefrog species. They have large eyes and respond very quickly to fast-moving insect prey. The fingers and toes are very well suited for gripping and straddling branches.

Sticky disc on toe used for gripping

Large eye

Finger helps treefrog grasp onto branch

Bright green colour as camouflage in trees

Large, red eye

NOT ALL TREEFROGS ARE GREEN
Treefrogs include some of the prettiest of all the frogs and can be any colour of the rainbow, like the painted reed frog (pp. 22–23). The yellow reed frog (above) from South Africa lives amongst lily pads in swampy areas. Poison-dart frogs (pp. 56–57) also live in treefrog-type habitats and have finger and toe discs, so they may also be thought of as treefrogs.

Straddling walk

RED-EYED TREE WALKER
This red-eyed treefrog is a capable climber which stalks its insect food. It is a "flying" frog and can glide between leaves and branches in its rainforest home. Red-eyed treefrogs are found in Mexico, Costa Rica, and Panama.

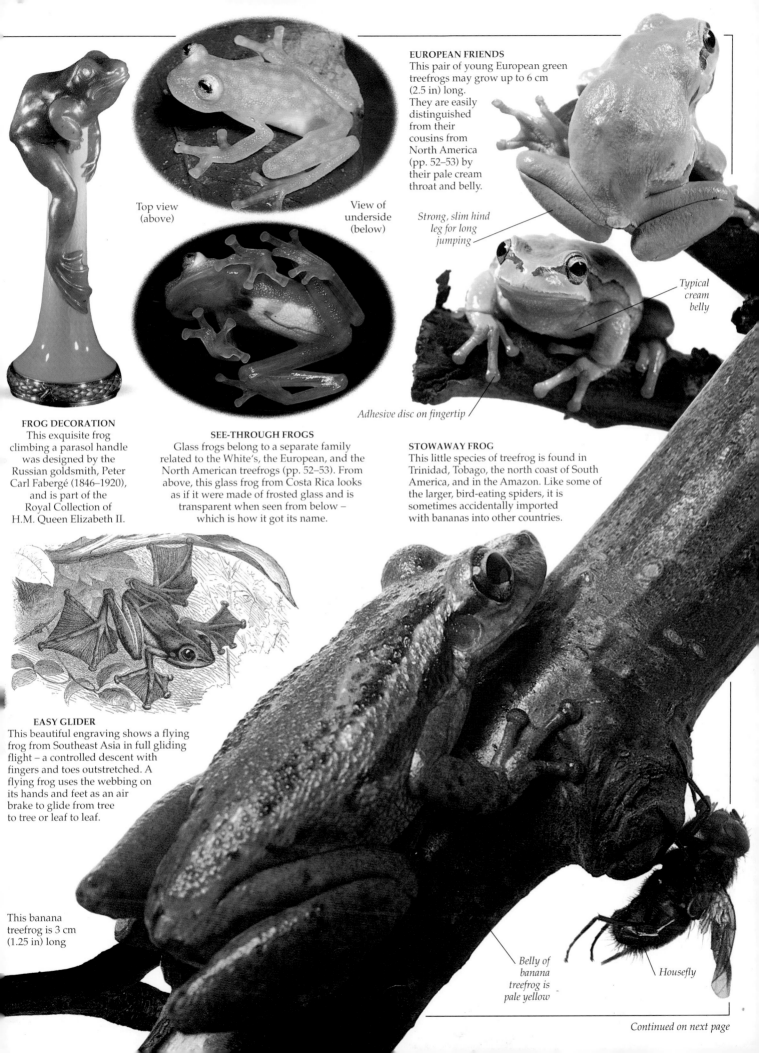

Top view
(above)

View of
underside
(below)

EUROPEAN FRIENDS
This pair of young European green
treefrogs may grow up to 6 cm
(2.5 in) long.
They are easily
distinguished
from their
cousins from
North America
(pp. 52–53) by
their pale cream
throat and belly.

*Strong, slim hind
leg for long
jumping*

*Typical
cream
belly*

Adhesive disc on fingertip

FROG DECORATION
This exquisite frog
climbing a parasol handle
was designed by the
Russian goldsmith, Peter
Carl Fabergé (1846–1920),
and is part of the
Royal Collection of
H.M. Queen Elizabeth II.

SEE-THROUGH FROGS
Glass frogs belong to a separate family
related to the White's, the European, and the
North American treefrogs (pp. 52–53). From
above, this glass frog from Costa Rica looks
as if it were made of frosted glass and is
transparent when seen from below –
which is how it got its name.

STOWAWAY FROG
This little species of treefrog is found in
Trinidad, Tobago, the north coast of South
America, and in the Amazon. Like some of
the larger, bird-eating spiders, it is
sometimes accidentally imported
with bananas into other countries.

EASY GLIDER
This beautiful engraving shows a flying
frog from Southeast Asia in full gliding
flight – a controlled descent with
fingers and toes outstretched. A
flying frog uses the webbing on
its hands and feet as an air
brake to glide from tree
to tree or leaf to leaf.

This banana
treefrog is 3 cm
(1.25 in) long

*Belly of
banana
treefrog is
pale yellow*

Housefly

Continued on next page

Continued from previous page

Male North American treefrog will call to attract a female of the same species

Bony head

Projecting bony upper lip

Sticky pad on end of finger

Head of duck-billed treefrog

DUCK-BILLED TREEFROG
Seen from the side, the head of this treefrog from Belize has a very unusual shape. The snout's bony ridges and "duck-bill" shape make the frog's head look very similar to that of the duck in this old engraving. They also make the frog look less frog-like and the bony ridges help to camouflage it against tree bark.

Cream strip from nose to tail

GREEN SONGSTER
Treefrogs are the song-birds of the amphibian world and their favourite calling sites are in trees high above the ground. The North American green treefrog has the tubby body shape, long hind legs, and sticky pads on the fingers and toes of a typical treefrog. Although many treefrogs look alike, differences in head shapes, colours, and markings are easily seen by comparing this treefrog with White's and European treefrogs (pp. 50–51).

GUESS WHO?
Kermit is probably based on the North American green tree-frog. Male treefrogs sing to attract their females – but not Kermit. He sings his love song to Miss Piggy!

A safe haven

The ancestors of modern tree-frogs were probably attracted to the safety of vegetation which was mostly free from predators and the more plentiful supply of insects which lived around the plants. Early treefrogs were probably better at grasping tall grasses, twigs, leaves, and leaf stems than other frogs. Many amphibians migrated from life on the ground to the surrounding vegetation above during the course of their evolution – particularly the frogs and toads (pp. 8–9). Many modern treefrogs are very vividly coloured. Seen away from their natural habitat, it is difficult to realize that their bright colours are used for camouflage (pp. 20–21), as well as for warning – or confusing – their enemies.

Skin's green colour helps treefrog merge into background

Dark markings on frog's back match tree bark

Unusual head shape helps with camouflage

BONE HEAD
The skin on the head of these two unusual treefrogs from Belize in Central America is fused onto the bony, box-like skull – this may help to reduce water loss (pp. 12–13). The treefrog protects itself from predators by backing into a hole in a tree trunk, using its head to block the entrance to its home.

Bony eyebrow protects eye (smaller than in most treefrogs)

Large, sticky, rounded disc on end of finger for gripping bark

1 FROM A SAFE PLACE
Against a leafy background this red-eyed treefrog would be well hidden. The green colour of its head, back, and legs, and the vertical stripes on its sides make it look like a leaf in dappled sunlight.

2 DANGER AHEAD
Jumping in trees is dangerous. A treefrog could easily hit (or miss) a branch, injure itself, or become tangled up in leaves or stems. Any movement is dangerous because it might also attract predators.

RED ALERT
This red-eyed treefrog from Central America is sitting in a typically alert treefrog posture. Treefrogs peer over the edges of leaves and branches to look out for both prey and predators, while hiding as much of themselves as possible (pp. 22–23).

Treefrog's eye typically facing forward

3 FULLY STRETCHED
The bright orange colour on the thighs and other normally hidden surfaces is an example of "flash coloration". A sudden flash of colour, combined with the jumping treefrog's unusual shape, confuses its enemies. When treefrogs land almost flat onto a leaf surface, they make a very quiet "slap" sound.

Flash colour of bright orange (but it can also be red, blue, or yellow)

Earth movers

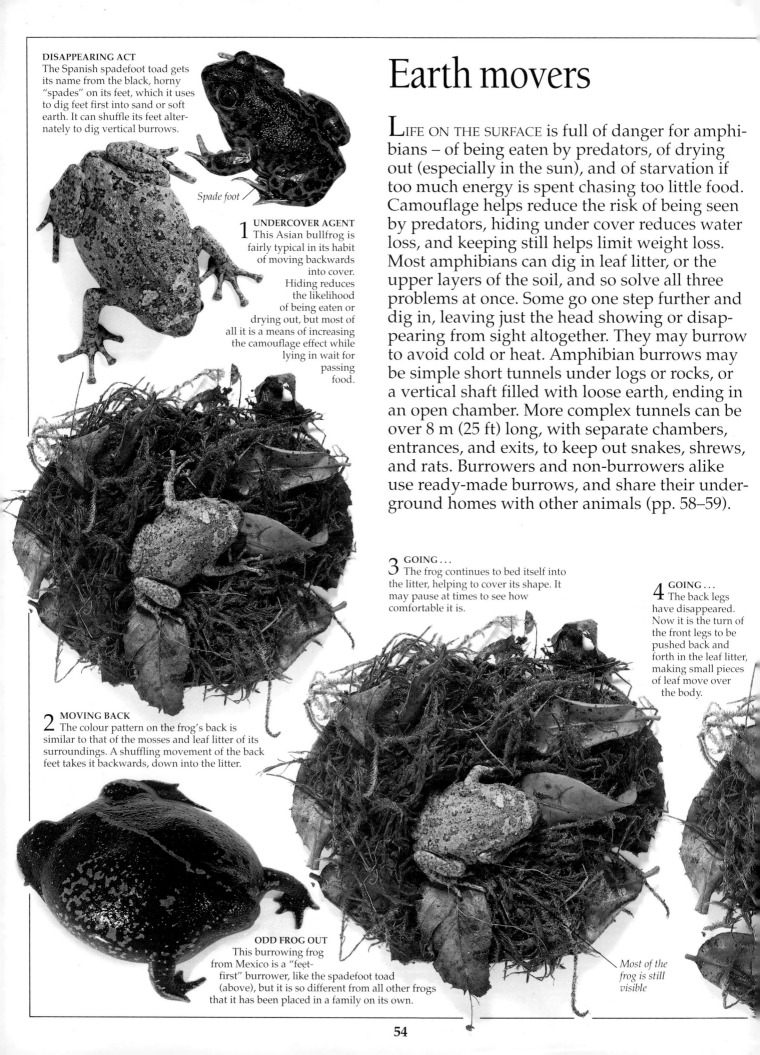

DISAPPEARING ACT
The Spanish spadefoot toad gets its name from the black, horny "spades" on its feet, which it uses to dig feet first into sand or soft earth. It can shuffle its feet alternately to dig vertical burrows.

Spade foot

1 UNDERCOVER AGENT
This Asian bullfrog is fairly typical in its habit of moving backwards into cover. Hiding reduces the likelihood of being eaten or drying out, but most of all it is a means of increasing the camouflage effect while lying in wait for passing food.

LIFE ON THE SURFACE is full of danger for amphibians – of being eaten by predators, of drying out (especially in the sun), and of starvation if too much energy is spent chasing too little food. Camouflage helps reduce the risk of being seen by predators, hiding under cover reduces water loss, and keeping still helps limit weight loss. Most amphibians can dig in leaf litter, or the upper layers of the soil, and so solve all three problems at once. Some go one step further and dig in, leaving just the head showing or disappearing from sight altogether. They may burrow to avoid cold or heat. Amphibian burrows may be simple short tunnels under logs or rocks, or a vertical shaft filled with loose earth, ending in an open chamber. More complex tunnels can be over 8 m (25 ft) long, with separate chambers, entrances, and exits, to keep out snakes, shrews, and rats. Burrowers and non-burrowers alike use ready-made burrows, and share their underground homes with other animals (pp. 58–59).

3 GOING...
The frog continues to bed itself into the litter, helping to cover its shape. It may pause at times to see how comfortable it is.

4 GOING...
The back legs have disappeared. Now it is the turn of the front legs to be pushed back and forth in the leaf litter, making small pieces of leaf move over the body.

2 MOVING BACK
The colour pattern on the frog's back is similar to that of the mosses and leaf litter of its surroundings. A shuffling movement of the back feet takes it backwards, down into the litter.

Most of the frog is still visible

ODD FROG OUT
This burrowing frog from Mexico is a "feet-first" burrower, like the spadefoot toad (above), but it is so different from all other frogs that it has been placed in a family on its own.

The South African spotted
shovel-nosed frog

6 GONE
Only
the head is
showing.
The frog
has gained a
major advan-
tage by its activity –
it is well concealed,
comfortable and
can reduce its
water loss, taking
up water through
its skin via contact
with damp soil and
leaves. By staying still,
it will not lose weight by
burning energy chasing after
food. All it has to do now is
wait for its prey to walk by.

HEAD FIRST
The spotted shovel-nosed frog from South
Africa is a "head first" burrower with a
difference – it actually uses its head, or
rather its snout, for burrowing. The body
is bent forward, head down, with the back
legs held straight, pushing the frog's snout
forwards into the soil. Digging is done by
raising and lowering the snout, scraping
soil away with its powerful hands. Other
head first burrowers, like midwife toads
(pp. 36–37) and mole frogs (pp. 44–45),
use only their hands and feet.

5 ABOUT TO GO
The legs and back half
of the body are now hidden.
The wriggling move-
ments continue;
the body is
rotated,
pushing it
down into
the leaf litter.

*Only the
frog's head
is visible*

Poison-dart frogs and mantellas

MANY AMPHIBIANS ARE BRIGHTLY COLOURED, but the most colourful of all are the poison-dart frogs from Central and South America and mantellas from Madagascar. These frogs use their bright colours to defend their territories from other males during courtship, as well as to warn predators that they are poisonous to eat. They have had to evolve more highly poisonous chemicals in their skin as their enemies, including snakes and spiders, are very resistant to milder skin toxins.

DANDY FROG
This exquisitely dressed frog, looking just like a poison-dart frog in his clothes of many colours, is all puffed up and in his Sunday best.

Bright colour helps to warn off predators

Red flash colour helps camouflage frog

This bright mantella has a red "flash" colour on the inside of its leg

This yellow mantella may be a colour variety of the green and black mantella (below), or a different species

STRANGE NAME
This species was originally given its common name because of its typical strawberry-red colour, made even brighter by deep blue-black flecks. Strawberry poison-dart frogs from different areas may have very different colours – blue, green, yellow, orange, plain, spotted, and even black and white.

WAR PAINT
Some native peoples of North America used war paint to strike terror into the hearts of their enemies. This Hopi Indian chief wears orange, red, and yellow – the classic warning colours – in his headdress. Amphibians also use the same colours to frighten away their enemies.

Identifying mantellas is very difficult – they have so many colour varieties (above)

Skin is highly toxic

GOLDEN LOOK-ALIKE
This golden yellow poison-dart frog looks very like its close relative – the more poisonous *Phyllobates terribilis* (pp. 60–61) – but it is smaller and has black markings on its legs.

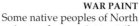

It has recently been discovered that the golden mantella from Madagascar produces the same kind of chemical poisons as South American poison-dart frogs

This green mantella (first described in 1988) is from Madagascar, where habitat destruction is a problem. It is important to know about new species so they can be protected (pp. 60–61)

Bright black and red stripes make this frog more visible, to warn off enemies

FASCINATING FROGS
Poison-dart frogs make up a fascinating group. Some are brightly coloured and highly poisonous, having complex chemicals in their skin. These frogs range in size from the very small (at 1.5 cm, or 0.6 in long) to larger ones (up to 5 cm, 2 in), like the two highly coloured frogs sitting on the leaves (right). Poison-darts are social animals, with complex territorial, courtship, and mating behaviours.

LIFE IN THE PENTHOUSE
This spotted poison-dart frog was discovered in 1984. It is found 15–20 m (48–65 ft) up in the treetops of the cloud forests of Panama. There may be many more high-level, tree-living species of amphibian waiting to be discovered.

POISONED DARTS
The Choco Indians, who live in western Colombia in South America, poison the tips of blow-pipe darts, which they use for hunting. They remove the toxin by heating the live frog over a campfire. Only a few species are used, but one is so poisonous (pp. 60–61), that the dart has only to be wiped against the live frog's back for it to be deadly.

Poison-dart frogs are social animals, living in small groups

HAWAIIAN HOLIDAY
This metallic green poison-dart frog from Costa Rica, Panama, and Colombia has been introduced into the islands of Hawaii and, like some of the other species, has also been bred in captivity.

When colours develop, the poison develops too

TOXIC TADPOLES
Poison-dart frogs carry their tadpoles to small isolated pools, often one at a time, where they develop their colours and skin poisons as they grow.

INSECT SIZE AND SOUND
This is one of the smallest poison-dart frog species (under 2 cm, 0.75 in). Discovered in 1980 in isolated patches of forest in the Andes Mountains, its scientific name means "buzzer" – after its insect-like call.

Yellow and black are warning colours, as in this poison-dart frog, and in the European fire salamander (pp. 14–15)

Friends and enemies

AMPHIBIANS HAVE FEW FRIENDS but many natural enemies, and are eaten by a wide range of animals. To survive, most amphibians have evolved superb camouflage colours and other means of defence (pp. 16–17). They also produce large numbers of eggs or have a special way of caring for their young. People are amphibians' worst enemy and threaten their survival with polluting and destroying their habitats. But some amphibian friends are animals that have dug burrows, unintentionally providing them with a home. Sometimes different species of amphibian will share a habitat or even burrow together. Other friends include people who try to protect amphibians and their environment (pp. 62–63).

THREATENED BY BATS
In tropical areas, bats have learned to home in on calling frogs, but bats do not have things all their own way. At least one species of frog in Australia (the common green treefrog) is known to eat bats.

FROGS VS. MICE
Ancient Greeks used animals in their fables to poke fun at political leaders. In this 16th-century engraving of the Trojan Wars, the frog-people won the war against the mice-people, when crabs nipped off the mice's legs.

A SECOND SKIN
Like other amphibians, the African dwarf clawed toad – a relative of the Surinam toad as well as the African clawed toad (pp. 22–23) – sheds its skin every five to seven days. This action possibly gets rid of parasites attached to the toad's skin.

Wrinkled skin starting to lift off and shed

Webbed feet make the clawed frog a powerful swimmer

MANY ENEMIES
As shown in this print by American artist, John James Audubon (1785–1851), many water birds, like these black-crowned night herons, eat vast numbers of frog. Other predators include spiders and large insects, as well as snakes, mammals, and larger frogs.

DOOM
In this fable by Aesop (620–560 B.C.), a mischievous frog tied a mouse to his foot. When the frog dived into a pool, the mouse drowned. A passing hawk ate both of them – the frog became a victim of his own prank.

INDOOR FROG
Many frog species share human homes, especially bathrooms, like this treefrog from Southeast Asia.

BEST OF FRIENDS
In western Europe, natterjack and midwife toads (left and centre in burrow) often share the same home. This may be a lifelong association between the two. Many other animals, like newts (right in burrow), also take advantage of the safe retreat of a ready-made burrow, with its food supply of earthworms, spiders, and beetles. The burrows may be up to 8 m (26 ft) long, with a shallow entrance of 15–25 cm (6–10 in) below ground.

TOAD AND FRIENDS
Frogs are popular figures on stamps. Here are Mr. Toad and his friends, Mole, Rat, and Badger, from the children's classic tale, *Wind in the Willows*, by Scottish-born Kenneth Grahame (1859–1932).

10½p

The Wind in the Willows
The Year of the Child

Rare and endangered

MANY SPECIES OF AMPHIBIAN ARE RARELY SEEN because they are secretive, like burrowing frogs, or because their natural habitat is inaccessible. Others are seldom found outside a small geographical area. Although amphibians new to science are still being discovered at the rate of 15 to 25 new species a year, many others are becoming rarer due to global warming, low water levels, pollution, acid rain, and the destruction of their habitats, such as cutting down rainforests or filling in ponds. Preserving natural habitats is the most important step in preventing these fascinating animals from becoming extinct.

MORE PRECIOUS THAN GOLD
This 2000-year-old, Chinese gold frog is valuable, but when a species disappears, it is gone forever!

Cream throat and belly

Tomato colour, but typical range from deep red to pale orange

Pair of tomato frogs from Madagascar, an island off the southeast coast of Africa

THE WORLD'S MOST POISONOUS FROG
First described as new to science in 1978, this bright yellow *Phyllobates terribilis* deserves its name. A poison-dart frog, which looks similar to *Phyllobates bicolor*, it is so poisonous that it could possibly kill a person.

The poisonous *Phyllobates terribilis* was discovered in Colombia

NEVER UPSET A SKUNK!
Skunks have an unpleasant defensive behaviour. If provoked, they spray a rotten-smelling liquid from glands at the base of the tail. The skunk frog (below) produces its evil smell from its skin, which exudes a thick mucus.

Skin, when touched, produces evil smell and thick mucus

Venezuela skunk frog

A BAD SMELL IN THE FOREST
The Venezuela skunk frog was described as new to science in 1991. It is the largest member of the poison-dart frog family (pp. 56–57), but its claim to fame rests on the very unpleasant odour which it gives off if it is in danger. Like its name-sake (above), the skunk frog uses its odour for defence, to drive away its enemies.

DISAPPEARING NEWT
The great crested newt is now on the protected species list in the UK – a special licence is necessary even to examine it in the wild. Twenty years ago, it was abundant all over Europe, but filling in home ponds and using agricultural poisons have taken their toll.

WILL THIS SALAMANDER SURVIVE?
The golden-striped salamander from northern Spain and Portugal depends upon natural brooks and streams for its larval development. The removal of large amounts of water for agricultural and human use has seriously threatened its survival.

A STEP IN THE RIGHT DIRECTION
These tomato frogs (left) are endangered, like many other frog species in Madagascar, but they are listed as an Appendix I species, which means they receive the highest level of protection in law. They have, however, been successfully bred in captivity. Captive breeding and the protection of the natural habitat as nature reserves may permit the reintroduction of this and other frog species back into the wild.

Great crested newt's tail is almost as long as its body

AN UNREPEATABLE PHOTOGRAPH?
Gatherings like this group of male golden toads (the females are olive-brown with bright red spots) in the Monteverde Cloud Forest Reserve in Costa Rica in 1985 may be a thing of the past. They have not been seen at all in this region since 1990.

ISLAND FROGS
This is Hamilton's frog, the rarest of three native species in New Zealand. It has been found only on two offshore islands in the Cook Strait. One population lives amongst a pile of rocks known as "Frog Bank" on Stephens Island, while a second, larger population lives in a small patch of forest on Maud Island. If rats were introduced by accident, especially onto Stephens Island, this rare frog could easily be wiped out in a very short time.

Typical stunning golden colour

UNDER THREAT
This golden mantella (pp. 56–57) from Madagascar is threatened by habitat destruction as are many other species of frog (and other animals) on the island. Madagascar has a high level of "endemism" – that is, most of its species are found only there and nowhere else in the world.

Conservation

HELPING HAND
Madagascan tomato frogs are endangered. They have been bred in captivity successfully, so if wild populations become extinct, they will still survive.

THE PROBLEMS people cause by destroying habitats such as cutting down rainforests, filling in natural ponds, taking water from rivers for industrial use, acid rain pollution, lowering the levels of fresh water, and global warming, all seriously threaten amphibian survival. People must change their attitude to the environment and its wildlife. Like all animals, amphibians have a right to live, undisturbed, in their natural habitat. Creating nature reserves, conserving natural habitats, and making places for amphibians in gardens and parks, will help ensure their continued survival. Studying, making new discoveries, and informing people about amphibians all help their conservation and show how important frogs, toads, newts, salamanders, and caecilians are in the beautiful natural world around us.

YOUNG NATURALIST
Caring young naturalists help to save amphibians, by raising tadpoles from frog-spawn and releasing them into garden ponds.

DOING TOO WELL!
Introducing foreign species into a country can be harmful – they may compete with the native amphibians. In 1935, the cane toad was introduced into Australia to control the cane beetle infecting the sugar cane. This toad has bred so successfully that it has become a serious pest in coastal areas of Queensland and northern New South Wales.

POND PREDATOR
Dragonfly larvae are found in ponds and streams. They are greedy predators and eat frog tadpoles and smaller newt larvae using their extended jaws. They should not be introduced into small ponds which contain amphibian larvae.

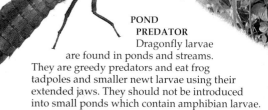

Frog tadpole

Pond snail keeps water free of too much algae

Tadpole feeding on a small piece of meat – it also eats boiled lettuce leaves

Newt larva feeds on water fleas

Water boatman

A TANGLE OF TADPOLES
Raising tadpoles from frogspawn and seeing them transform into small adults is fascinating. Sensitive to pollution and acid rain in fresh water, tadpoles are good indicators of change in the environment.

Waterweed provides oxygen to keep pond water fresh

Newt larva develops front legs first, but frogs develop hind legs first

Fringing plants and logs provide cover for adult amphibians

Natterjack toad lives in heathlands and sand dunes

RARE TOADS
The natterjack toad is a protected species in the UK. Its continued survival depends on carefully managing its habitats.

WATER BOATMAN
This insect swims upside-down in the water, using its large, oar-like back legs, and it also eats tadpoles!

FEEDING SNAILS
Watch how snails feed, compared with tadpoles reared in a tank. They both rasp away at algae-covered surfaces and aquatic plants.

GARDEN PONDS
Garden ponds (above) are vital to the survival of amphibians. A garden pond can be made quite cheaply using a black polythene, or butyl rubber, liner. The pond should have shallow and deep areas and it should be as large as possible. In the northern hemisphere the pond should be at least 60 cm (2 ft) deep, to prevent it freezing solid in winter.

Waterweed provides oxygen, food, and cover for tadpoles

Rubber liner – up to 60 cm (2 ft) deep

Index

Acknowledgements

Dorling Kindersley would like to thank:
Peter Hayman of the British Museum, Harry Taylor of the Natural History Museum, and Michael Dent (London) for additional special photography. Dr. Gerald Legg, Jeremy Adams, and John Cooper of the Booth Museum (Brighton); the British *Dendrobates* Group; Peter Foulsham of the British Herpetological Supply; Ken Haines; David Bird, Myles Harris, Fiona MacLean, and Robert Stephens of Poole Aquarium; Regent Reptiles; the Reptile-arium; and Roger Wilson of the Rio Bravo Field Studies Centre (Belize), for providing species information and specimens for photography. The staff of the British Museum (especially Lesley Fiton,

Catharine Harvey, Sarah Jones, Richard Parkinson, Peter Ray, and James Robinson), and the Natural History Museum (especially Ann Datta, Dr. Angela Milner, and Tim Parmenter) for their research help. Doris Dent and Alan Plank for providing props for photography. Alex and Nicola Baskerville, and Amy Clarke as photographic models. Manisha Patel, Sharon Spencer, and Helena Spiteri for their design and editorial assistance.
Jane Parker for the index.

Illustrations Joanna Cameron

Picture credits
t=top, b=bottom, c=centre, l=left, r=right
Zdenek Berger: 8tc.
Biofotos: Heather Angel 23tl, 35br, 37tl;
Brian Rogers 37tcr.
Prof. Edmund D. Brodie Jr.: 16bcr, 17bcr, 36bc, 47cr, 49c, 49bl, 56c.
Dr. Barry Clarke: 20bcl, 23tc, 50cl.
Bruce Coleman Ltd: John Anthony 61tr;
Jane Burton 16tr; Jack Dermid 16tc, 49cb;
Michael Fogden 36bcl, 37bcr, 61cr;
Jeff Foott 60cr; A.J. Stevens 55tl, 55cl.
Dorling Kindersley: Frank Greenaway 38tl, 38tr, 38b, 39tr, 39cr; Colin Keates 8b, 9tc, 9tr; Dave King 11tl; Karl Shone 7tr; Kim Taylor and Jane Burton 39cl, 39b; Jerry Young 12tr, 20bl, 23tr, 30cl, 44cr, 50b.
Mary Evans: 14tl, 32tl, 36tr, 46cl, 48tr, 56tl, 57cr.
Copyright Jim Henson Productions, Inc.
Kermit the Frog is a trademark of Jim Henson Productions, Inc.

All rights reserved: 52tr.
Image Bank: Al Satterwhite 21br.
Kobal Collection: 34bc.
Mike Linley: 13tr, 17bl, 17cl, 20bcl, 32tcl, 32bcl, 32cr, 32bl, 33bc, 36tcl, 54t.
Musée Nationale d'Histoire Naturelle: 8tr, 9tl.
C.W. Myers, American Museum of Natural History: 57tcl, 57cl, 60bl, 60bc.
Motoring Picture Library, National Motor Museum at Beaulieu: 6tl.
Naturhistoriska Riksmuseet: 8c.
NHPA: ANT 44tr, 61bl; Stephen Dalton 25cl, 27bl; Jany Sauvanet: 29cr, 46cb.
Oxford Scientific Films: Kathie Atkinson 13tl, 13tc; Jim Frazier 13r; Michael Fogden 22tcr, 51tc, 51c; Z. Leszczynski 7cl.
Royal Collection, St James's Palace, copyright Her Majesty the Queen: 46tr, 51tl.
Paul Verrell: 34c.
Zefa: 56cr; K. & H. Bensor 19bcl.

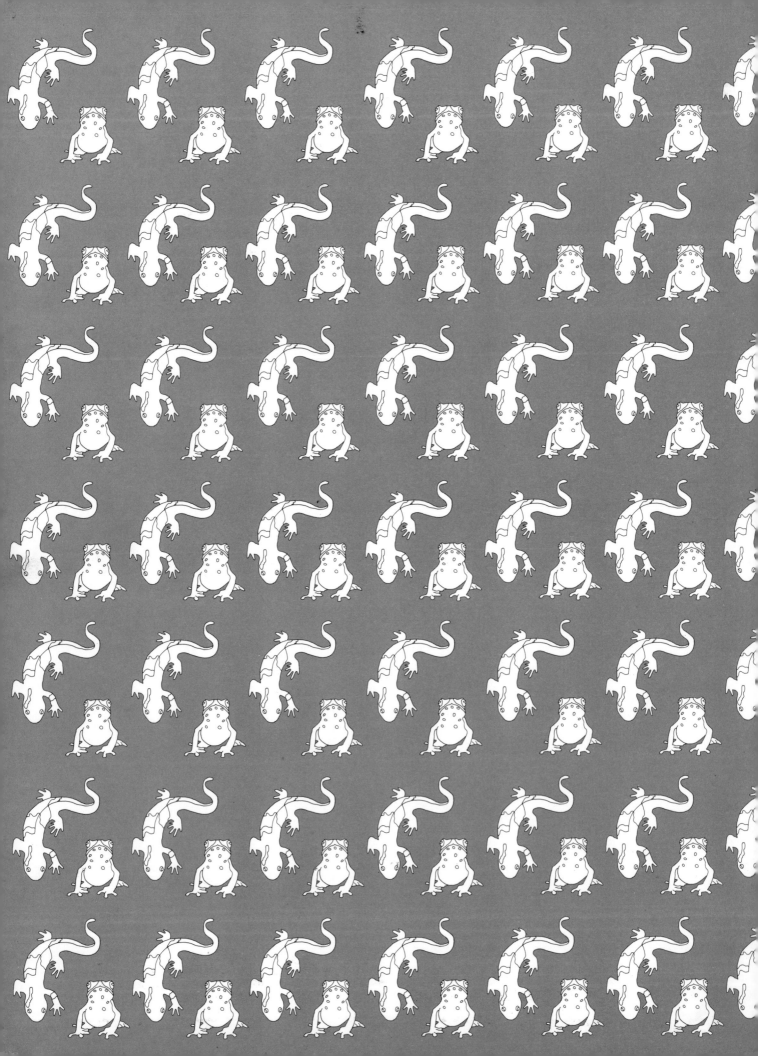